Sharing
Cities
ACTIVATING the
URBAN COMMONS

Edited by Shareable

Creative Commons

First Edition: 2018

ISBN
Print Edition: 978-0-9992440-0-5
Ebook (ePub, PDF, word version): 978-0-9992440-1-2

www.shareable.net

Printed by Lightning Source (Ingram). Environmental paper sourcing information can be found here: https://www.ingramcontent.com/publishers/resources/environmental-responsibility

Photos on book cover, from left to right starting from top left corner:

BOOK AT A GLANCE

CHAPTER 1: HOUSING / 40

Cooperative Housing, Short-term Rental Policy, Accessory Dwelling Units, Tiny Houses for the Homeless, Open-source Design, Community Renewal.

CHAPTER 2: MOBILITY

Ride Hailing, Cooperative Taxi, Walking School Bus, Car Sharing, Shared Mobility Strategy, Bike Sharing, Mobile Transit Platform.

CHAPTER 3: FOOD / 82

Kitchen Library, Surplus Food Redistribution, Community Gardens, Peer-to-Peer Food Sharing, Urban Orchards, Farmers Markets, Urban Agriculture Incentive Zone.

CHAPTER 4: WORK / 103

FabLabs, Cooperative Ownership, Community Wealth, Platform Cooperatives, Makerspaces, Arts Cooperatives, Social Entrepreneur Networks.

CHAPTER 5: ENERGY / 124

Community Choice Aggregation, Wind Energy Cooperative, Purchasing Alliance, Shared Ownership of Renewable Energy Infrastructure, Feed-in-Tariffs.

CHAPTER 6: LAND / 143

Community Land Trusts, Placemaking, Reclaiming Public Land, Open Land Data, Public Art and Culture, Peer-to-Peer Space Rental, Foreclosure Fine Ordinance.

CHAPTER 7: WASTE / 165

Citizen Compost Initiative, Repair Café, Worker-owned Recycling Cooperative, Zero-Waste, Municipal Reuse Center, Open-source Benchmarking.

CHAPTER 8: WATER / 183

Remunicipalisation, Community Bill of Rights, Community-led Management, Depaving Public Space, Community Science, Resident-managed Sanitation.

CHAPTER 9: TECHNOLOGY / 206

Internet for All, Crowdsourced Data, Managing Response to Disasters, Open-source Software, City Making, Open-data Policy, Addressing the Digital Divide.

CHAPTER 10: FINANCE / 227

Credit Unions, State Banks, Local Currencies, Community Benefits Agreements, Civic Crowdfunding, Civic and Elder-care Time Banking, Citizen Investment in Local Food Systems.

CHAPTER 11: GOVERNANCE / 251

Urban Commons, Participatory Budgeting, Civic Project Software Platform, Participatory Planning, Polycentric Planning for Climate Change, Neighborhood Partnership Network.

SHAREABLE STAFF

Neal Gorenflo
San Francisco, U.S.
@gorenflo
Executive editor and contributor
Neal is the co-founder and executive director of Shareable who believes in the power of sharing.
http://www.shareable.net/users/neal-gorenflo

Tom Llewellyn
San Francisco, U.S.
@shareabletom
Project manager, editor, and contributor
Tom is the strategic partnerships director at Shareable.net, and a lifelong sharer, commoner, and storyteller.
http://www.shareable.net/users/tom-llewellyn

Maira Sutton
San Francisco, U.S.
@maira
Editor and contributor
Maira is a writer and organizer focused on the intersection of human rights and the commons, who works as the community engagement manager at Shareable.
http://www.shareable.net/users/mai-sutton

Ambika Kandasamy
Boston, U.S.
@ambikakandasamy
Editor
Ambika is a journalist and digital strategist who works as the managing editor at Shareable.
http://www.shareable.net/users/ambika-kandasamy

Joslyn Beile
San Francisco, U.S.
Business manager and editor
Joslyn is the operations manager at Shareable, responsible for organizational initiatives to sustain Shareable's mission.
http://www.shareable.net/users/joslyn-beile

FELLOWS

Adrien Labaeye
Berlin, Germany
@alabaeye
Land and Technology fellow
Adrien is a researcher in Berlin working on commoning at the intersection of urban and digital spaces.
http://www.shareable.net/users/adrien-labaeye

Daniel Araya
Champaign, U.S.
@danielarayaxy
Editing fellow
Daniel has a doctorate from the University of Illinois and is a researcher and government adviser.
http://www.shareable.net/users/daniel-araya

Darren Sharp
Melbourne, Australia
@dasharp
Work and Waste fellow
Darren is the director of Social Surplus, a strategy consultancy that works with governments and communities to activate Sharing Cities. He is the Australian editor of Shareable and Melbourne coordinator of the Sharing Cities Network.
http://www.shareable.net/users/darren-sharp

Emily Egginton Skeehan
Tokyo, Japan
Energy and Water fellow
Emily is a marine scientist working for the Japan Agency for Marine-Earth Science and Technology in Yokosuka, Japan.
http://www.shareable.net/users/emily-skeehan

Khushboo Balwani
Brussels, Belgium
@khushbooBalwani
Food and Work fellow
Khushboo is a designer and strategist working on how collaborative methodologies can solve social challenges in India and in Europe.
http://www.shareable.net/users/khushboo-balwani

Kristen Hewitt
Northampton, U.S.
@kristen0wl
Production fellow
Kristen is a writer and editor living in western Massachusetts.
http://www.shareable.net/users/kristen-hewitt

Leila Collins
New York, U.S.
@LeilaCollins4
Mobility and Finance fellow
Leila previously worked on the collaborative economy movement in Israel and the West Bank and currently works at a PropTech accelerator in New York City.
http://www.shareable.net/users/leila-collins

Marco Quaglia
Rome, Italy
@MarcoQuaglia89
Waste and Governance fellow
Marco is a former member of LabGov with experience in the NGO sector; he lives in Rome, Italy, where he currently works in management consulting.
http://www.shareable.net/users/marco-quaglia

Nikolas Kichler
Vienna, Austria
Housing and Water fellow
Nikolas works as a researcher at the Vienna University of Technology, exploring ways to widen opportunities for citizens to co-create their cities.
http://www.shareable.net/users/nikolas-kichler

Ryan T. Conway
Bloomington, U.S.
Technology and Governance fellow
Ryan is a political economist and community organizer with a passion for the democratic self-organization and ethic of stewardship found frequently in the establishment and endurance of community commons.
http://www.shareable.net/users/ryan-conway

Ryan Gourley
Ann Arbor, U.S.
@ryangourley
Editing fellow
Ryan serves as director of the University of Michigan student venture accelerator, and is an educator and entrepreneur working to bring social innovations to life.
http://www.shareable.net/users/ryan-gourley

Sharon Ede
Adelaide, Australia
@sharonede
Housing and Mobility fellow
Sharon is an urbanist and activist who works to build the sharing and collaborative movement in Australia and beyond.
http://www.shareable.net/users/cruxcatalyst

Simone Cicero
Rome, Italy
@meedabyte
Collaboration fellow
Simone is a strategist and designer who has been exploring collaborative productions models for more than a decade. He is also the creator of the Platform Design Toolkit and OuiShare Connector.
http://www.shareable.net/users/simone-cicero

Wolfgang Hoeschele
Heidelberg, Germany
Energy and Finance fellow
Wolfgang lives in Heidelberg, Germany, and focuses his efforts on developing strategies toward a truly sustainable economy – an "economy of abundance of life."
http://www.shareable.net/users/wolfgang-hoeschele

CONTRACTORS

Copy Editing and Proofreading:
Ellie Cabrejas Llewellyn
http://www.etc.plus

Book Layout and Design:
The Public Society
http://thepublicsociety.com

Cover Design:
Juni Xu and Laurissa Barnes-Roberts

ADDITIONAL CONTRIBUTORS

Housing:
Harry Knight (WikiHouse Foundation).

Food:
Anna Davies, Marion Weymes, and Oona Morrow (SHARECITY and Trinity College Dublin); Myriam Bouré (OuiShare and Open Food Network Community).

Work:
Juan Manuel Aranovich and Agustín Jais (Club Cultural Matienzo); John Duda (The Democracy Collaborative); Nathan Schneider (University of Colorado Boulder); Mayo Fuster Morell (dimmons.net and Berkman Klein Center for Internet and Society, at Harvard University).

Energy:
Ana Marques (ICLEI) and Toni Pujol (Barcelona City Council); Elana Keef (Afri-Coast Engineers SA); John Farrell (Institute for Local Self-Reliance).

Land:
Cat Johnson (freelance journalist, Shareable); Anna Bergren Miller (freelance journalist, Shareable); 596 Acres; Rob Poll-van Dasselaar and Joris Goos (City of Rotterdam).

Water:
Ben Price (Community Environmental Legal Defense Fund); Heartie Look (Waterkeeper Alliance); Della Duncan (Upstream Podcast), Eric Rosewall (depave); Johannes Euler (Das Commons Institute); Michael O'Heaney (Story of Stuff).

Technology:
Freifunk Münster group.

Finance:
Matt Stannard and Marc Armstrong (Public Banking Institute).

Governance:
Anna Bergren Miller (freelance journalist, Shareable); LabGov.

SUPPORTERS

Bologna, Italy, workshop participants:
Michel Bauwens (P2P Foundation), Christian Iaione (LabGov), Silke Helfrich (Commons Strategies Group), David Bollier (Commons Strategies Group), Oriana Persico (Art is Open Source), Salvatore Iaconesi (Human Ecosystems Relazioni srl), Sheila Foster (Fordham University), Jay Walljasper (On the Commons), Paula Z. Segal (596 Acres), Amy Cahn (Public Interest Law Center), Cristina Zurbriggen (Universidad de la República), Aiichiro Mogi (Ritsumeikan Asia Pacific University), Jeff Andreoni (journalist), and Claudio de Majo (researcher).

Shareable Advisory Board:
Laurie Schecter (Shift Foundation), Michael Stoll (SF Public Press), Tony Lai (Legal.io), Julian Agyeman (Tufts University), and Catherine Homicki (Dartmouth College).

We would also like to thank the countless people who offered guidance and support along the way, including all of our partners, advisers, Sharing Cities Network organizers, and readers.

This project was made possible by a generous grant from the Shift Foundation, to whom we are incredibly grateful.

Das Commons Institute

Freifunk Münster Group

I C L E I Local Governments for Sustainability

9

CONTENTS

6
LAND
145

9
TECHNOLOGY
206

7
WASTE
165

10
FINANCE
227

8
WATER
185

11
GOVERNANCE
251

CHAPTER 1: HOUSING / 40

CHAPTER 2: MOBILITY

CHAPTER 3: FOOD / 82

CHAPTER 4: WORK / 103

CHAPTER 5: ENERGY / 124

CHAPTER 6: LAND

CHAPTER 7: WASTE / 165

CHAPTER 8: WATER / 185

CHAPTER 9: TECHNOLOGY / 206

CHAPTER 10: FINANCE / 227

CHAPTER II: GOVERNANCE / 251

INTRODUCTION

By Neal Gorenflo

"Sharing Cities: Activating the Urban Commons," is a collection of 137 case studies and policies in 11 categories that demonstrate that a city run by the people is not only possible, but that much of it is already here. From participatory budgeting in Brazil to resident-managed public spaces in Italy to taxi cooperatives in the U.S., there's almost no service that can't be run democratically by citizens for each other.

With the backdrop of worsening income inequality, climate change, and fiscal challenges, the growth of self-organized, democratic, and inclusive means for city dwellers to meet their own needs by sharing resources couldn't be more relevant. These cases and policies taken together offer a new vision for cities that puts people – not the market, technology, or government – at the center, where they belong. Moreover, the book represents a claim on the city by people – a claim increasingly being made by city-residents the world over. This book was written for a broad audience, but may find special resonance with those who share this people-first vision of cities and want to act on it. Written by a team of 15 fellows with contributions from 18 organizations around the world, "Sharing Cities: Activating the Urban Commons" not only witnesses a movement, but is a practical reference guide for community-based solutions to a range of challenges cities face such as affordable housing, sustainable mobility, and more.

THE START OF A MOVEMENT

On May 7, 2011, Shareable, the nonprofit media outlet I co-founded two years earlier, hosted a daylong conference called Share San Francisco at the Impact Hub coworking space in the city. We brought together 130 leaders from city government, nonprofits, and social enterprises to explore one key question, "How can we amplify the city of San Francisco as a platform for sharing?" We wanted to learn how San Franciscans could share more when they already shared a lot. After all, cities are fundamentally shared enterprises.

We hoped to catalyze positive change from a set of opportunities coalescing around cities – some particularly evident in San Francisco, where Shareable is based. What has transpired since has gone well beyond our expectations. It all started with a conversation around a few observations that by themselves are important, but have world-changing potential if managed together for the common good.

The keynote speakers – including Lisa Gansky, entrepreneur and author of "The Mesh," Jay Nath, at the time San Francisco's Director of Innovation, and myself – framed the opportunity for sharing in cities around the following observations:

- Humans had only recently become a globally-connected, urban species with more people living in cities and owning a cellphone than not. We've only just begun to tap the potential of a new situation.

- In an era of gridlocked, ideologically-driven politics, cities are where change is still possible, as exemplified by pragmatic, solutions-oriented leadership we see in issues like climate change.

- With the rise of extremely low-cost production technologies and highly efficient, coproduction methods, producing things could become far more democratic and distributed geographically. Dependence on multinational corporations for goods and services could be greatly reduced.

- Cities are more energy efficient per capita than nonurban areas, thus mass adoption of collaborative models of production and consumption could dramatically improve that efficiency.

- If managed correctly, these trends could turn cities into great places to live for everyone while addressing challenges that threaten our species' very existence, like climate change, wealth inequality, and social division.

- Government, business, and civil society all have a role to play and have to work together to realize this opportunity.

I illustrated the potential impact with car-sharing, which had already been studied extensively by Susan Shaheen and her team at the University of California, Berkeley's Transportation Sustainability Research Center (TSRC). TSRC's 2010 survey of North American car-sharing members showed that one shared car replaced up to 13 owned cars, and 51 percent of members joined to gain access to a car when they previously did not have access to one. A separate estimate by the National Building Museum showed that for every 15,000 cars taken off the road, a city could keep $127 million in the local economy. Not surprisingly, the large majority of spending on cars ends up in the coffers of multinational corporations.

As I concluded in my keynote at the event, there aren't any other innovations I know of that can dramatically increase access to resources, boost the local economy, and reduce resource consumption simultaneously. I asked participants to imagine the whole economy organized around access rather than ownership, and the huge impact that might result from such a transformation.

In any case, we did our best to make the case that sharing and cities offered a unique, world-saving opportunity. The message became cornerstone of the global Sharing Cities movement that started to unfold shortly after Share San Francisco.

In San Francisco, city officials showed immediate interest. Nath wanted to learn more. Over the next six months, we shared our knowledge with him, connected him to more local sharing entrepreneurs, and discussed how to grow the local sharing movement. He eventually asked Shareable to host an educational roundtable for Mayor Ed Lee about the sharing economy and organize the public launch event for a new city government task force called the Sharing Economy Working Group (SEWG), which was to take point in formulating sharing-related regulations.

Milicent Johnson, Shareable's community organizer at the time, took the lead in organizing the SEWG launch event, which was held April 3, 2012, at SPUR, San Francisco's urban policy think tank. Mayor Lee, the president of the board of supervisors David Chui, and I gave the keynote talks, along with other leaders from various sectors. After the keynotes, I moderated a panel featuring local sharing entrepreneurs, including Joe Gebbia of Airbnb, Jessica Scorpio of Getaround, and Leah Busque of TaskRabbit, all soon to be white-hot focal points of the global sharing-economy phenomenon. Gabriel Metcalf, executive director of SPUR, later told us that it was the most attended event in SPUR's 100+ year history. Much to our surprise, the event also garnered significant worldwide press coverage.

Just six months later, Mayor Park Won-soon of Seoul, South Korea, launched Sharing City Seoul, at least partly inspired by San Francisco's SEWG. In contrast to SEWG, Sharing City Seoul (described in more detail in Chapter 4) had more substance. It was launched as a substantial package of policies and programs with the goal to mainstream sharing in Seoul, and in the process, address Seoul's most pressing problems including unemployment, pollution, and social isolation. It had funding, a multiyear implementation strategy, numerous citizen-stakeholders, and the city's 60-person innovation department behind it.

However, Sharing City Seoul's importance to the Sharing Cities movement goes far beyond its instructive details. It is Mayor Park's signature program for a mega-city of 10 million people. Moreover, Seoul is part of a small cadre of the world's largest, most modern cities that are defining what a city is in the 21st century. In this context, Mayor Park decided to tell a new story about what a city can be, a story that diverged significantly from the usual talk of cities as competitors in a ruthless global market. Instead, he focused attention on a practical, interpersonal action – sharing – that ordinary residents can engage in to help each other and the city as a whole. Unlike some efforts, it's a genuine extension of Mayor Park's career as a human rights lawyer, social justice activist, and social entrepreneur – someone who clearly saw the great human and environmental toll his city has paid in catapulting itself from a backwater to one of the world's most modern cities in one generation.

For these reasons, Sharing City Seoul became the single biggest catalyst of the global Sharing Cities movement and earned Mayor Park the prestigious Gothenburg Award for Sustainable Development in 2016. Its impact has been immense. It has inspired dozens of cities to start similar programs:

- In Europe, the London-based SharingCities.eu consortium is working with London, Milan, Lisbon, Warsaw, Burgas, Bordeaux, and other Sharing Cities projects. Netherlands-based ShareNL has long worked with Amsterdam (the first European Sharing City) and is now reaching out to many more cities in Europe and beyond through their newly-formed Sharing City Alliance. The P2P Foundation has recently completed an urban commons transition strategy for the city of Ghent. Last year, the Paris-based nongovernmental organization OuiShare co-hosted Sharing Lille, a multifaceted festival attended by over 1,000 people meant to foster more sharing in Lille, France. The 2017 theme of the organization's flagship Paris event – OuiShare Fest – was cities. In addition, its far-flung members are working with numerous cities on sharing projects through its network in Europe and South America.

- In Asia, the Sharing Economy Association of Japan (SEAJ) is currently developing Sharing Cities programs with 26 rural municipalities in Japan. Last year, five Japanese cities – Chiba, Yuzawa, Taku, Hamamatsu, and Shimabara – unveiled plans, developed with SEAJ, to foster more sharing. And, of course, the movement has taken off in South Korea. On Nov. 6, 2016, at Seoul Sharing Festival, which I attended as a member of Mayor Park's Sharing Economy International Advisory Group, seven Korean cities – Seoul, Jeonju, Suwon, Seongnam, Siheung, Gwangju, and Don-gu – signed a joint declaration announcing their plans to develop their Sharing Cities programs together.

This is just a start at outlining the movement. It's hard to judge its scope and size because, like many movements, there is no central organizing body and its boundaries are somewhat fuzzy. I've only mentioned cities that we know of – and our network has its limits – that self-identify as a Sharing City or have a Sharing Cities program. There are also other cities – such as Bologna, Barcelona, Frome, and many more – that do not use the label "Sharing City" to de-scribe projects or development strategies where sharing, the commons, and coproduction play a central role.

In addition, there are many efforts that we consider part of the movement that do not involve a city government. For example, there's ShareCity, a large, university research project led by scholar Anna Davies studying food-sharing enterprises in 100 cities from around the world. There's Friends of the Earth UK's Big Ideas project, which catalyzed Duncan McLaren and Julian Agyeman's groundbreaking book, "Sharing Cities: A Case for Tru-ly Smart and Sustainable Cities." There are also cities like Port-land that have a rare concentration of grassroots sharing projects including clothing swaps, lending libraries, and shared workspac-es. Sharing Cities are part of, and intersect with, a much larger and more diverse set of efforts by people working toward sus-tainability, democracy, and shared prosperity in cities.

As the Sharing Cities movement unfolded, Shareable catalyzed it further through continuous news coverage, publishing the first ever Sharing Cities policy guide, "Policies for Shareable Cit-ies," in 2013, and launching our Sharing Cities Network. Togeth-er, this helped grow the movement, particularly among local activists and politicians in the U.S. and Europe. The Sharing Cities Network, an events network Shareable started in 2013, was crucial not only to this effort, but to this book. The idea for it came from network members.

A BOOK IS BORN

When we decided to create this book, we also decided to walk our talk by creating it collaboratively. We assembled a team of 15 fellows from nine countries (see the Contributors page for their biogra-phies) to crowdsource the book proposal and write the book. We officially launched the project January 20, 2016. Simone Cicero, our collaboration fellow from Rome, Italy, ran what became an extended visioning process to create a shared understanding of the purpose, structure, and content of the book. This was done through a series of video conferences. It resulted, after much deliberation, in a book proposal that everyone unanimously supported. The extra time spent on the visioning process was well worth it considering the book proposal's clarity.

The team decided to create a collection of short, accessible, and proven or promising case studies (of programs, projects, or enterprises) and model policies (laws, regulations, or city plans) that support sharing in cities. We decided to organize the cases and policies by 11 functional areas of a city such as housing, food, and transportation, and curate about six of each per chapter. Each chapter is the product of two fellows who together selected and wrote the cases and policies. In addition, 18 organizations contributed articles including ICLEI, Story of Stuff, and Club Cultural Matienzo (see the Contributors page for the list of participating organizations).

The collection not only illustrates the vision of a Sharing City through examples, but also communicates the book team's core belief. We believe that it's possible to run much of a city on a commons basis, that a city could be in nearly every way of, by, and for the people, and that the urban commons is, as Silke Helfrich pointed out in her IASC Urban Commons Conference keynote in 2015, a "concrete utopia." In other words, a credible utopia that's well within reach because its parts already exist, though they've not yet been assembled in one place to make a complete Sharing City. The team wanted the book to represent this concrete utopia and serve as an assembly manual for it, or at least a start at one.

While the selections were curated by the book fellows, they aren't offered in a dogmatic spirit. We don't presume to be the final authority on what constitutes a Sharing City. We see ourselves as contributing to a dialogue, and imperfectly so. This is a reference book, so you can use whatever is relevant. Most of the material in it can stand independently. The book is designed to be modular so that it can be excerpted, remixed, and otherwise remade as you like. In fact, all the material is Creative Commons and available as a text file, so you can literally curate your own book from this book.

It's also an unfinished work. We've imagined it as the kernel of an open-source project that requires a community to fully flesh it out. Or as version 1.0 of limitless versions, because we've only scratched the surface of what's in a dynamic, growing field. There's so much more that deserves to be widely recognized. Raising awareness needs to be an ongoing community effort. One of the lessons I learned while working on this book is that there's a blindness to the power people have to meet their needs outside of the market and state (the commons option), which is made more poignant because we need this power now more than ever. Hopefully, this book opens many eyes to what's abundant as leaves of grass in a vast plain. Perhaps it's human nature to overlook what's always around us. To live in a city is to be completely enveloped by what is shared, from sidewalks and streets to parks and squares to space and time itself. So I strongly encourage you to expand this catalogue of hope.

WHAT'S ACTUALLY IN THE BOOK? CIVIC IMAGINATION INSIDE

There are 69 case studies and 68 model policies in this book. Though the book only scratches the surface of what's out there, the geographic and sectoral diversity of our selections will expand your view of what's possible. Together, they are provocative in the best possible way. In terms of the case studies, I challenge you to flip through the book and not be amazed at what ordinary people can do when they commit to projects where personal interests and the common good are aligned. The case studies undermine the myth that "there is no alternative" to capitalism – TINA for short – and show that "there are many alternatives" – known as TAMA in the commons world.

Take, for instance, RideAustin, a nonprofit Uber alternative described in Chapter 2 that has raised $8 million in donations, facilitated over 1 million rides, raised $100,000 for local charities through its app, and is on track to be self-sustaining through an innovative funding model, all without charging drivers anything. Along similar lines is COOP Taxi in Seoul (Chapter 2). Seoul supported the development of this new taxi service that combines convenient ride-hailing technology with driver ownership and control of the business. These are just two of many examples that prioritize community and/or worker control over a global, investor controlled option that extracts as much revenue as possible out of the hundreds of cities it serves. Why should a city risk dependence on a startup that extracts money from the local economy when it can cultivate options that keep money circulating in it?

Also consider Club Cultural Matienzo (CCM, Chapter 4), formed in 2008 in the wake of a tragic nightclub fire that killed 194 people and triggered a wave of club closings that throttled Buenos Aires' grass-roots arts scene for years. CCM innovated a safe, legal, profitable, and worker-controlled business model for cultural spaces. Its support helped the number of local venues grow by 800 percent (from 100 to 800) in nine years. Today, these clubs buy supplies together to reduce costs, host multi-location festivals, and lobby the city for arts-friendly policies. The result is a safer, vibrant arts scene that supports artistic talent at a mass scale while creating decent jobs for young workers. This is far cry from the commercial club scene that all too often exploits artists, workers, and fans with little regard for over-all vibrancy of a community's arts scene. In Buenos Aires, grassroots culture is supported as a commons.

The model policies are exciting in their own way. As legal tools, they open space for the kinds of projects highlighted by our case studies. Most, like the ghost tax regulation in London (to reduce vacant hous-ing), peer-to-peer parking regulation in Montreal (to increase supply of parking in crowded areas), and open land data policy in Rotterdam (to manage land better), are solutions aimed at addressing specific challenges. However, there are a few policies that are multifaceted and represent a new commons-based paradigm. This includes Cuba's agricultural model (Chapter 3), Barcelona's policies for the "commons collaborative economy," which is made of 120 crowdsourced policy ideas to create a more fair, local sharing economy (Chapter 4), and the regulatory foundation of Seoul Sharing City (Chapter 4). Another paradigm-shifting standout is Bologna's Regulation on Collaboration Between Citizens and the City for the Care and Regeneration of the Urban Commons (see Chapter 11), which allows citizens to no longer be passive recipients of city services, but active agents in shaping public life for the better. It provides a legal framework and administrative process by which citizens can directly care for urban commons such as parks, streets, cultural assets, schools, and much more. It fills a gap in administrative law that doesn't allow citizens to maintain or create public assets and services in cities.

The book also covers some expected territory – how cities should regulate Airbnb (Chapter 1) and Uber (Chapter 2). However, it might surprise you that our book fellows' interest in this aspect of Sharing Cities was surprisingly low. It was more of a box to check. The book team felt that while it's important to reorient aggressive commercial actors toward the commons, the more game-changing innovations are commons-based from the beginning.

There were many challenges in selecting the case studies and model policies even though our crowdsourced book proposal set out clear standards – that they be commons-oriented, city-based, and easily-replicable. For instance, there are few cases and policies that are purely commons-oriented. The majority of the pieces have a commons element, and the rest arguably set the stage for commons development. For instance, Barcelona's Solar Thermal Ordinance (Chapter 5) helps to localize renewal energy production, setting the stage for a commons approach to energy, but doesn't imagine a commons in its effort to promote sustainability.

The scale requirement was also a challenge, because sectors like energy, water, and waste have critical regional and national dimensions. This sometimes made it difficult to find solutions that were discretely city-based. In addition, many cases did not fit snugly into the categories the team chose. This was particularly true of the broad, paradigm-shifting policies – like Seoul

Sharing City – which seek impact in a variety of areas. This was a lesson in the intertwined nature of different socio-geographic scales, the inadequacy of siloed approaches to resource management, and the need for whole-systems thinking in urban design.

This should give you a taste for what's in the book. These are days when city residents need options, especially as established institutions all too often fail to exercise what urban commons scholar Christian Iaione, a Bologna regulation co-author, calls "civic imagination."

CONTENT IN CONTEXT

The commons was part of, but not the core of, our Sharing Cities vision when we hosted Share San Francisco in 2011. This changed pretty quickly for two reasons. First, it was clear that Sharing Cities could easily be co-opted by commercial interests to help promote a technological vision of cities or simply be subsumed under the corporate smart cities rubric. We had experienced this kind of co-optation firsthand with the sharing economy. We chronicled the birth of the sharing economy in San Francisco starting in 2009, but once billions of dollars in venture capital started to flow into these once fragile and communitarian-minded startups, the concept of sharing became a moral cover for a particularly aggressive extension of business as usual. When this happened, our reporting turned critical on the Silicon Valley version of the sharing economy. We also began to frame sharing in relation to geographic-bounded communities through our Sharing Cities reporting and activism to reduce the chance of co-optation. Still, the risk remains.

Second, and most importantly, we benefited greatly from ongoing collaboration with a community of commons theorists including Michel Bauwens of the P2P Foundation, Silke Helfrich and David Bollier of the Commons Strategies Group, Christian Iaione of LabGov (who co-wrote the Bologna regulation), law scholar Sheila Foster of Georgetown University, and others. Over the last few years, they've worked within a wider network of stakeholders to flesh out a commons-based political economy for cities through a global program of research, public communication, and civic laboratories. We at Shareable were fortunate to have participated in some of this work, but we mostly reported on it. We did this because we not only saw their work as groundbreaking, but also believed it could help define and defend a people-first vision of cities. We felt that any such vision of cities, Sharing Cities or otherwise, needed its own political economy or it would simply melt into the corporate grid, no matter how good the intentions. That's what our experience with the sharing economy taught us.

THE URBAN COMMONS

The importance of the urban commons to cities today is that it situates residents as the key actors – not markets, technologies, or governments, as popular narratives suggest – at a time when people feel increasingly powerless. To paraphrase commons scholars Sheila Foster and Christian Iaione, the city as a commons is a claim on the city by the people. Furthermore, a commons transition is a viable, post-capitalist way forward, as the groundbreaking fieldwork of the P2P Foundation in Ecuador and the examples in this book suggest.

But what is the commons and why is it a credible alternative? David Bollier's excellent primer, "Think Like a Commoner," gives a good definition.

According to Bollier, the commons is:

> *A self-organized system by which communities manage resources (both depletable and replenishable) with minimal or no reliance on the Market or State.*

> *The wealth that we inherit or create together and must pass on, undiminished or enhanced, to our children. Our collective wealth includes the gifts of nature, civic infrastructure, cultural works and traditions, and knowledge.*

> *A sector of the economy (and life!) that generates value in ways that are often taken for granted — and often jeopardized by the Market-State.*

Importantly, as Bollier points out, the commons is not merely a re-source and the people who use it. The most important component is the relationship between a resource and its users, which is embodied in the user-managed governance arrangements that regulate access.

The commons is a credible alternative or augmentation of state and market resource management because it's been used for hun-dreds, if not thousands, of years. An estimated 2 billion people rely on it today, mostly in rural areas. It's also been extensively studied. Nobel Laureate Elinor Ostrom's decades of research on the com-mons contain a message that couldn't be more relevant today – that commons-based resource management is often more efficient and long-lasting than state or market approaches. This book benefit-ed greatly from the contributions of Ryan T. Conway, a member of the Ostrom Workshop at Indiana University, a legendary center for commons research since 1973. The policy he contributed about poly-centric planning for climate change in Dortmund, Germany (Chapter 11), goes even further. It reflects Ostrom's belief that a decentralized, local approach to climate change could be more effective in aggre-gate than current global approaches.

While the commons is a promising approach to urban challenges, the study of the commons has historically been focused on relatively isolat-ed, rural, natural resource commons like irrigation systems, fisheries, and forests. In comparison, research on urban commons is fairly new. It remains to be seen if the commons can become the new, dominant par-adigm for resource management – as some commons activists posit – in a place like the city where all the forces of society come to bare.

Still, we at Shareable believe that the commons needs to be elevated to a dramatically higher level of importance in urban development, but not to the exclusion of the state and market. Instead, the three spheres of commons, state and market must be put on a peer basis institution-ally, harmonized, and managed to control the excesses and foster the strengths of each. We don't think government or markets are inherent-ly good or bad. They, like any institution, including the commons, can be guided to serve or degrade the common good.

As such, commoners must build *and* fight, to borrow from the strategy of Cooperation Jackson. We must build the urban commons and reform the government and market. The commons can't thrive if the government and market are hostile to them, which largely is and has been the case historically speaking. Moreover, cities need strong, socially responsible versions of all three spheres to become truly resilient. Coral reefs are famously resilient because every function in the ecosystem is managed by numerous species in different ways. Similarly, cities need a heterodox political economy to thrive. This is a job for the finest versions of all our tools. Simply replacing a free market orthodoxy with a commons-based one is not the way forward. As Elinor Ostrom herself once said, "No panaceas!" In other words, no simple, one-size fits all formulas, and that goes for the commons too. It's not the answer to everything.

In this way, a Sharing City is less a thing and more a mindset and a dynamic, participatory process characterized by the below principles, and perhaps more:

- **Solidarity.** Sharing Cities represents a revived story about cities that recognizes community as the heroic protagonist in urban transformation. Aristotle, the leading philosopher during Athens' golden age, believed that the city existed for the well-being of its people. In this story, people work together for the common good rather than compete for scarce resources. This age-old wisdom challenges popular narratives that portray high technology and competitive markets as heroes in the story of cities. A Sharing City is of, by and for all people no matter their race, class, gender, sexual orientation, or ability. In other words, Sharing Cities are primarily civic, with residents focused on taking care of each other, their city, and partner cities too. Their primary function is to produce residents capable of working together for the common good, the foundational skill that makes all other things possible in society. Looking forward, and to paraphrase the Buddhist monk Thích Nhất Hanh, the next Buddha will be community. A multitude of loving, human-scale communities managed by capable residents is how we'll protect all life on earth. The solution is us.

- **Distributed architecture.** Sharing Cities support a commons-oriented shift from an industrial model of urban development, which centralizes the various functions of a city in separate zones for batch processing by bureaucracies, to a networked architecture, which distributes functions throughout the city for real-time processing through open networks. The distributed model is characterized by mixed-use zoning, modular architecture, event-based use of multifunction assets, and on-site processing of energy, water, and waste. It also enables new ways to manage resources (access over ownership) and multiple types of currencies (fiat, local, reputation) and property (public, private, and community). If managed democratically, Sharing Cities' distributed architecture has the potential to dramatically increase the health, wealth, and resource efficiency of all city residents.

- **Private sufficiency, civic abundance.** To quote George Monbiot, "There is not enough physical or environmental space for everyone to enjoy private luxury... Private luxury shuts down space, creating deprivation. But magnificent public amenities – wonderful parks and playgrounds, public sports centres and swimming pools, galleries, allotments and public transport networks – create more space for everyone, at a fraction of the cost." Civic abundance should include public schools, spacious squares, expansive walkable cityscape, extensive bikeways, lending libraries, Fab Labs, pocket parks, coworking spaces, cultural centers, child care co-ops, food pantries, and more. In fact, each neighborhood should have a mix of civic amenities tailored to their needs. Sharing Cities are a path to abundance and celebration, not deprivation and drabness that downscaling consumption often suggests.

- **Common needs, co-designed solutions.** Sharing Cities focus on common needs and pragmatic, community-developed solutions as opposed to top-down, one-size-fits-all solutions. This requires co-design, experimentation, learning, and iteration by the community. It also requires avoiding unnecessary replication of divisive national politics at the local level, which can take the focus off common needs and solutions. To paraphrase Father Arizmendi, the founder of Mondragon cooperative: ideologies divide, common needs unify.

- **Transformation over transaction.** Sharing Cities emphasize solutions that build residents' ability to work together. This is preferable to solutions that reduce provisioning to mere economic transactions. Services that build collaborative capacity can produce transformative social goods, lead to new collaborations, and help put a community on a positive, long-term trajectory. As in the case of northern Italy, a strong civic culture can last for centuries and is a precondition for long-term shared prosperity. Moreover, this emphasis creates space for individuals to develop as human beings. As Desmond Tutu has said, "a person is a person through other persons." We need each other to become fully human.

- **Local control, global cooperation.** Sharing Cities create many democratic, local centers of power that cooperate globally. This cooperation can take many forms. For instance, city governments could develop an open-source urban commons technology stack together. Think Airbnb and Uber, but with locally-owned, democratically-controlled instances of services that are also connected through a global platform. This is what futurist José Ramos calls "cosmo-localization." It's a strategy to achieve scale while building solidarity.

- **Impact through replication, not just scale.** Sharing Cities can systematically encourage the documentation of local solutions so they can be adapted and replicated in other places. Here, solutions are only loosely connected. This process requires minimal technology and administrative investment. Scale is not the only path to dramatic impact. Both scale and replication strategies should be pursued.

- **Cross-sector collaboration, hybrid solutions.** To thrive, the urban commons must adapt to the dense institutional web of the city. Unlike isolated rural commons, urban commons have no choice but to negotiate mutually beneficial relationships with government and the market. This must happen at the project and city scale as demonstrated by Bologna's urban commons and the Co-Bologna project. Sharing Cities' solutions are often hybrids of the commons, government, and market.

- **Systems thinking, empathy.** City residents, urban planners, local politicians, and single-issue advocates need to become more aware of how different functions within a city interact with each other and are shaped by the surrounding region. For instance, the impacts of land use, transportation, housing, and jobs on each other are profound. There is an increased need for them to be planned together, and at a regional scale. Stakeholder groups must have empathy for one another and co-design urban solutions that optimize for the whole, not just one or a small cluster of issues or jurisdictions.

- **Build *and* fight.** Sharing Cities must seize the immediately available opportunities for commons development. Many commons projects need little if any funding or permission to start. While political change is necessary, it's unwise to depend solely on or wait passively for it. Today's urgent challenges require immediate action. That said, a completely independent, parallel economy is not possible. The urban commons need to be fought for politically too, and that takes long-term vision and commitment. To borrow from Cooperation Jackson's strategy, we must build and fight for Sharing Cities.

- **Competitive advantage through quality of life, security, and distinctiveness.** Sharing Cities are great places to live because they foster healthy relationships and natural environments, top contributors to health and happiness. Sharing Cities enhance social and environmental resilience. In an increasingly unstable world, the advantages of a supportive community and an accessible resource base represent an attractive safety net. In addition, Sharing Cities are distinctive because the commons preserve local culture and tradition. This distinctiveness helps them compete globally. The best cities will increasingly be known by the unique, and even transformative, experiences they make possible. The 21st century version of cathedrals, which drew millions of people to European cities during the Middle Ages, will be the uplifting social interactions, safety, and everyday joy experienced in Sharing Cities. As the old Irish proverb goes, it is in the shelter of each other that the people live.

What principles would you add?

A CALL TO ACTION

This is no time for mere resistance. Nor is it time for blame, resignation, or sharpening our differences. It is time for bold, new visions. It is time to reach across boundaries, identify common needs, and work together to meet them directly where we live. It is time for pragmatic solutions by the people. It is time for human beings to go on new, creative adventures together as if our lives depended on it, because they do.

This call to adventure in cities must be answered. There, "the fierce urgency of now," to quote Martin Luther King Jr., is felt acutely. Soul searing, society-rending levels of inequality, racism, pollution, and social isolation are the daily lived experience of billions of city dwellers, now making up over half the world's population. Yet, cities remain places of great hope. There, the potential for change is as abundant as suffering. Cities are simultaneously leading us toward and away from the brink of extinction. They are rising faster than nations to meet global challenges like climate change – at the same time they are the key drivers of such systemic problems. We live in a new age of cities, but the human future has long been forged in cities, the cradles of civilizations and arguably our species' most important and durable social innovation.

The future, however, is never assured. It must be made together. We must decide together what kind of cities we want to live in and what kind of people we want to become. We are more knowledgeable than ever about what makes a great life and what brings out the best in human beings. Our power to shape the conditions that shape us has never been greater. So, there may be no more important question than this: How can we turn cities from impersonal engines of destruction into intimate communities of transformation?

The global economic crisis woke many up to the realization that prioritizing economic growth over all life on planet Earth is the source of the multiple crises we face and not a solution as some establishment politicians stubbornly insist. As the recent shifts in global politics suggest, there's growing agreement among ordinary people that the status quo is failing us.

WHAT NOW?

To paraphrase commons scholar Keith Taylor, when markets and governments fail, we have us. In other words, we have a largely unacknowledged ace up our sleeves, another way to provision our lives that puts us in control – the commons.

Let's use it.

SHARING CITIES

This map is a visual representation of a small slice of the fast-growing, global sharing movement. The pins on the map show the locations of the case studies and policies in this book.

HOUSING   ENERGY   **TECHNOLOGY**

MOBILITY   LAND   FINANCE

FOOD   **WASTE**   GOVERNANCE

WORK   WATER

HOUSING

Affordable, quality housing is a human right. It is one of the elements that form the basis of cohesive, stable societies. Yet in many of the world's cities, housing affordability is slipping further out of reach of the average citizen, partly due to wages not keeping pace with the cost of housing and partly as a result of property speculation.

The typical response to a lack of affordable housing is a call to build more housing. However, in many cities, there are a number of dwellings that lie vacant, while people remain on waiting lists for public housing, are thrown into competition in tight rental markets, or become homeless. If there is already vacant housing stock, simply building more houses will not necessarily address the dynamic that keeps them vacant while people are in need of housing.

In some parts of the world, housing is kept affordable and renters have long-term rights and protections, which means they have effectively the same tenure as homeowners. Models such as community land trusts offer more affordable options for getting into the housing market. In other places, the move to downsizing, cohousing, self-built, and tiny house options are adaptive responses to an unaffordable housing market.

Policy responses in such a complex area as housing need to be both well thought out and applied in order to ensure they achieve their objectives. There are also approaches – that are simpler and can be readily enacted – to offer relief for those who cannot secure affordable housing, such as a "financial signal" built into rates that incentivizes owners to rent their properties. Housing is a human right. Secure, affordable housing is also a foundational requirement for a healthy, functioning society, and the economic fortunes of a city.

Sharon Ede

Humanitas:
Senior Care Meets Student Dorm in Shared Intergenerational Living

♀ Deventer, Netherlands

By Sharon Ede

PROBLEM

Students are increasingly finding that accommodations near college campuses are substandard or unaffordable. Meanwhile, older people in care often experience social isolation, which studies demonstrate adversely impacts both their mental and physical health.

SOLUTION

Humanitas Retirement Village, a long-term care facility, offers free accommodation to students in exchange for 30 hours of their time per month to help the older residents. Currently, six students are residents in the village. This arrangement provides a mutual benefit: rent-free accommodation for students and a younger demographic to help support the care of, and foster interactions with, older residents.

As part of their volunteer agreement, students teach residents various skills – such as using email and social media – and provide companionship. While these exchanges are important, it is living in such proximity that helps relationships and connections develop, eases loneliness, and makes a positive contribution to the mental health of the seniors.

"The students bring the outside world in, there is lots of warmth in the contact."

Gea Sijpkes, head of Humanitas

Source: PBS News Hour

RESULTS

- Two more senior care homes in the Netherlands have adopted the Humanitas model.

- There are similar intergenerational-living programs in other cities like Lyon, France, and Cleveland, Ohio, in the U.S.

RESOURCES

- Humanitas website: www.humanitas.nl/rver-ons/about-humanitas

- CityLab article: www.citylab.com/housing/2015/10/the-nursing-home-thats-also-a-dorm/408424

Opportunity Village Eugene:

A Transitional Microhouse Community Addressing Homelessness

⚲ Eugene, Oregon, U.S.

By Sharon Ede

PROBLEM

A range of factors can contribute to people becoming homeless, including economic downturns, rising costs of housing, cuts to Social Security and health care, and personal circumstances like a health crisis and relationship breakdowns. People who find themselves homeless can be vulnerable, especially at night. The city of Eugene, Oregon, has a population of approximately 160,000 with an estimated homeless population of 3,000.

SOLUTION

Opportunity Village Eugene (OVE) is a "tiny house" community that provides secure accommodation for around 35 people who were previously homeless. OVE provides residents with more than just affordable shelter – being part of the village offers the dignity of having a private space and access to a shared laundromat, kitchen, bathroom, and workshop. Residents also receive quarterly bus passes and have access to computers and Wi-Fi to help bridge mobility and digital divides.

The community requires some reciprocity from its members. Residents contribute $30, help with cleaning and maintenance, and participate in managing the community. OVE

"People look at the unhoused in our communities and think it's a shameful thing. For me, the shameful thing is that we, as a society, have not made it possible for the poorest of the poor to live with any dignity."

Dan Bryant, executive director of Opportunity Village

Source: Future Perfect

has a no drug or alcohol use policy, which means that, while the space does create a safe community for residents, it excludes homeless people who are struggling with substance abuse.

There is no limit to how long someone can stay at OVE. However, residents are encouraged to develop their personal plan for moving to more permanent accommodation, finding work, or whatever their path forward entails.

While OVE is not a panacea for homelessness, it is a working model that can be replicated to support people who need housing immediately and give them breathing room to transition into more permanent housing. The willingness of the local authority to support the OVE project has been a key factor in its success, for two reasons in particular:

- The city gave the project a plot of land and a 12-month lease, which they subsequently voted unanimously to extend for two more years.
- None of the tiny homes met the city's code for a dwelling or a residence, but they were given an exemption after a safety inspection.

RESULTS

- OVE has provided housing for more than 90 people since it was established in 2013.
- In the organization's report to the city on their first-year pilot, OVE's board revealed that the entire project of 30 dwellings and amenities was delivered with $100,000 cash and an equivalent amount of materials and other in-kind support. The upfront cost of providing a bed for a night was $12; however, as OVE's initiator, urban planner Andrew Hebden noted that "if you amortize the construction cost over five years, assume the same operating costs as our last quarter for the remaining four years, the cost of operating the village comes to less than $3/bed/night. In other words, for less than $3/night, we are providing safe and decent shelter for 35 members of our community."

RESOURCES

- Opportunity Village Eugene: http://www.squareonevillages.org/opportunity
- Shareable article: www.shareable.net/blog/eugene-tiny-house-villages-model-innovative-solutions-to-homelessness

Mietshäuser Syndikat:
Fosters Self-organized Housing Projects

⚲ Multiple Locations, Germany

By Nikolas Kichler

PROBLEM

The founders of "Mietshäuser Syndikat" (tenements syndicate), a network of cohousing projects in Germany, observed many self-organized cohousing projects struggle and fail. Some couldn't overcome the challenges in the critical early phases, in terms of dealing with legal issues, finances, and group dynamics, while others created commercially-exploited housing projects against their original intentions. At the same time, many cohousing projects did not have the capacity to support each other.

SOLUTION

The Mietshäuser Syndikat was launched to support self-organized, social housing projects. It connects successful, established projects with emerging ones to provide help, while at the same time reducing re-commercialization by ensuring all inhabitants co-own all real estate assets of all cohousing projects.

A legal construct stipulates that each cohousing project is considered an autonomous enterprise that owns its real estate, with the legal status of a limited liability company (LLC or "GmbH" in German). This GmbH consists of two partners: the cohousing association itself and the Mietshäusersyndikat GmbH. The form of limited

"Actually, we should not even exist, since already our basic approach violates the rules of the market: profit mongering, capital investment, and acquisition of private property are considered the indispensable basis for all economic enterprises. But we exist — the Syndikat and the projects — and we are among them: we cavort in the urban undergrowth among building speculators and property sharks, among home-builders, apartment owners, building associations, and capital investment firms."

syndikat.org

liability companies allows the property assets to be interconnected, since decisions cannot be made unilaterally. Finally, the single associate of the network's GmbH is the MHS Association, which all inhabitants are part of.

For a cohousing initiative to join MHS, some requirements must be met: The cohousing project needs to be self-organized by its residents, and a house and a financing plan must be on hand. Once the cohousing project establishes a secure financial basis, it needs to support new projects that are in the critical, cost-intensive early phases, the same way it received help when it began. The MHS Association represents all inhabitants of all cohousing projects and has a veto right when it comes to reprivatization and commercial exploitation of individual projects. Regarding any other issue concerning the residents, loans, rents, and renovation, the co-residents themselves make decisions on behalf of their own cohousing association.

RESULTS
- Since 1983, the network has grown to consist of 111 cohousing projects with a total of about 3,000 residents.
- Twenty-one initiatives throughout the country are in the process of joining the network.
- Spin-offs like "habiTat" in Linz, Austria, have been established in other countries.

RESOURCES
- The Mietshäuser Syndikat: www.syndikat.org/en
- Habitat (German): habitat.servus.at

CoAbode:

Matching Compatible Single Mothers for Cohousing

◌ Multiple Locations, U.S.

By Sharon Ede

Many single mothers work tirelessly to ensure they have good, affordable housing, while they hold down a job and take care of their children on their own. With around 40 percent of single parents in the U.S. employed in low-wage jobs, single mothers experience high rates of poverty even as they work long hours. Sharing the financial and practical responsibilities of housing, rather than struggling alone, can help make life easier. CoAbode is a service that matches compatible single mothers for shared housing, as well as services and support to make parenting less challenging. Cohousing can result in the mothers sharing their food and child care; it reduces financial costs, frees up time, and enables mutual support. Membership is free, and with 120,000 members registered, there are CoAbode members in many U.S. cities including Brooklyn, San Diego, and Washington DC.

RESOURCES

• CoAbode: www.coabode.org

WikiHouse:
Open-source Home-building Project

♀ Worldwide

By Harry Knight *(WikiHouse Foundation)*

Cities are struggling to meet the housing needs of an urbanizing society, while also focusing on the environmental and economic resilience of their community. WikiHouse is an open-source building project that is working to make it much simpler for anyone to design, manufacture, and assemble beautiful and sustainable homes that are suited to their needs. The goal is to help cities shift from a reliance on a centralized industrial economy to a more distributed, democratic, and scalable industry. It is a way to give citizens and communities the tools to produce, procure, and operate sustainable and affordable homes themselves.

Through many contributions and innovations, the WikiHouse community created an open and shareable building system called "Wren." It was used to build their first home in the English midlands. They hope to expand and build upon this first phase by creating a platform that will enable homeowners, small businesses, and others to work collectively to fabricate and build homes where they are needed most.

RESOURCES
• WikiHouse: www.wikihouse.cc

Babayagas House:
Self-managed Cohousing for Seniors

Paris, France

By Sharon Ede

Many countries share the challenge of how to support an aging population. Current models of senior care can be expensive, unsustainable, and unappealing to those living longer active lives. Aging women in particular tend to have limited options, since many do not have financial savings due to having had low-wage jobs or unpaid caring work throughout their lives. The Babayagas House, in eastern Paris, is a self-managed social housing initiative. It was established by a group of older women who wished to maintain their independence by living together in a supportive community. Residents pay an affordable rent for their own small apartments and share the cost of a monthly visit by a health care professional. There are around 21 women aged 66 to 89 living in the six-story house – a third of whom live on the poverty line. Seniors have replicated the Babayagas model in other cities across France and Canada.

RESOURCES
- Radio France Internationale article: en.rfi.fr/france/20130305-babayagas-house
- Senior Planet article:
  seniorplanet.org/senior-housing-alternatives-urban-cohousing-the-babayaga-way

Embassy Network:
New Collaborative Housing Model for Purpose-driven Young Professionals

⚲ Worldwide

By Neal Gorenflo

Young urban professionals frequently face high housing costs, social isolation, and career-building challenges. Embassy Network, one of the pioneers of the global coliving movement, addresses all three in a new shared-housing model. Properties in the network house from five to 20 people each. They include converted mansions, retreat centers, and small hotels. Residents share food expenses, regular communal meals, commons space, cars, and most importantly, career support. They are typically social entrepreneurs, freelancers, and young professionals seeking to make a positive impact through their work. Embassy Network creates an encouraging environment for personal and career development through peer support, regular public events, short-term visitors who share knowledge, and access to all nine Embassy Network properties located in North America, Central America, and Europe.

RESOURCES

• Find a coliving community here: coliving.org

• Embassy Network: embassynetwork.com

Equitable Regulation of Short-term Rentals

San Francisco, California, U.S.

By Sharon Ede

Digital platforms like Airbnb, Flipkey, Stayz, and many more have made it easy for city residents to offer spare rooms, or even entire residences, to those (most often tourists) needing short-term rental (STR) accommodations. STRs are typically defined as stays under 30 nights.

STRs bring with them a range of benefits, including helping residents generate extra income from unused spaces, opening up accommodation in areas where there's unmet demand, serving as overflow capacity when hotels are full, bringing visitors to areas of the city which don't attract high levels of tourism, and generally stimulating local economic activity.

There are also important drawbacks, especially in cities where such platforms have achieved a high level of market penetration. Public policy issues begin to emerge, such as the loss of hotel-related municipal revenue, health and zoning violations, safety concerns, noise complaints, and, perhaps most importantly, a decline in affordable rental housing stock. In a growing number of cases, owners evict long-term tenants to rent their houses to more profitable short-term guests, or speculators buy or lease residential real estate to set up illegal hotels.

The Sustainable Economies Law Center (SELC) in Oakland, California, has produced a guidebook for equitably regulating short-term rentals entitled, "Regulating Short-term Rentals: A Guidebook for Equitable Policy." The gist of the guide is to legalize some aspects of STR activity, while ensuring the public interest is protected. The guide covers areas of concern for hosts, guests, communities, and local governments, including protection of affordable housing supply, ensuring the well-being and safety of guests, respecting the rights of neighbors, ensuring public tax revenues are maintained in ways that are fair to short-term rentals and commercial hotels, and ensuring reporting and recordkeeping.

SELC suggests that policymakers consult the guide for general principles, but tailor the recommendations to each city's particular circumstances in dialogue with all local stakeholders. The guidebook was released in 2016, so it is yet to be adopted by a city in its entirety. However, a number of municipalities have developed local ordinances aligned with the guide. For example, Lisbon recently joined Paris, Amsterdam, and a number of U.S. cities in signing an agreement with Airbnb for responsible home sharing, while enabling Airbnb to collect and remit tourist taxes to the city on behalf of hosts.

VIEW THE FULL POLICY

- drive.google.com/file/d/0B1VPWTZ0vw6MTVh2b182QTFVV1E/view

RESOURCES

- Amsterdam's December 2016 Airbnb agreement: www.amsterdam.nl/publish/pages/813509/agreement_amsterdam_and_airbnb_mou.pdf

- Shareable's take on Amsterdam's Airbnb agreement – it's not tough enough: www.shareable.net/blog/amsterdam-updates-agreement-with-airbnb-to-combat-illegal-hotels-but-is-it-enough

- NY Times story on New Orleans' Airbnb deal, touted as the new, tougher model for cities to follow: www.nytimes.com/2016/12/07/technology/new-orleans-airbnb-model.html

I Love my Neighborhood ('Quiero mi Barrio') Community Renewal Program

◊ Multiple Locations, Chile

By Nikolas Kichler

The Chilean Ministry of Housing and Urban Planning subsidized 2 million houses between 1990 and 2005 to counteract long-lasting housing deficits. Despite its overall success, other qualities, such as social cohesion and the opportunity for residents to co-create their neighborhood, were neglected. In many areas, this resulted in social segregation, stigmatization, and other social problems. To address these challenges, the federal government initiated a national program called "Quiero mi Barrio" (I Love My Neighborhood) to help residents and their local organizations to think of city development as a collaboration between them and municipalities. The program's goals also include strengthening the social fabric, emphasizing the collectivity of neighborhood life, and generally improving neighborhoods' physical condition.

The program consists of three main phases that were implemented during a period of two to four years. Two hundred communities from around the country were chosen based on urbanity, population, social vulnerability, and other factors.

In the first phase of the program, Neighborhood Development Councils (NDC), consisting of local residents and social organizations, were established. The NDCs provided a place for debate about community visions, priorities, and goals. The results of these community debates were memorialized in Neighborhood Contracts, a public commitment to carry out projects they had agreed on. In phase two, NDCs monitored the implementation process and helped ensure goals were met, while community organizations provided necessary tools, budget and technical assistance. During the last phase, the projects were evaluated and future challenges outlined. The NDCs and municipalities drew up Future Agendas to establish long-term working relationships.

The program reached 3 percent of the Chilean population. Much was learned by all stakeholders, especially on how to plan and act together.

VIEW THE FULL POLICY

- www.minvu.cl/incjs/download.aspx?glb_cod_nodo=20061113165715&hdd_nom_archivo=DS_14_07_ACT_21_11_07.pdf

RESOURCES

- Quiero mi Barrio website (Spanish): quieromibarrio.cl

The Ghost House Tax:
Bringing Vacant Houses Back to Life

London, U.K.

By Sharon Ede

When speculators in residential real estate drive up prices, it can create a more transient population or trigger a local population decline. This can undermine the social and economic vitality of an area. Local economic and social dynamics such as retail patronage, school enrollments, and the diversity of the local community often change for the worse.

In 2012, over 6 percent of homes in the London borough of Camden were unoccupied on a full-time basis. The vast majority of these properties were second-home investments rather than owner-occupied residences. According to a May 2016 article in The Guardian, the borough reflects a London-wide phenomenon. Reports suggest Vancouver, Sydney, and San Francisco suffer similarly.

Though a "ghost house" tax could be seen as imposing on private decisions, it is in fact a counterbalance to an existing policy and rent-seeking regime that favors speculators. This regime allows speculators to seek capital protection and appreciation by "parking" wealth in residential real estate investments.

Bringing ghost houses "back from the dead" was a policy priority for Camden, and in December 2012, the Borough approved a policy to charge an extra 50 percent in property tax rates to owners of houses that had been unoccupied for more than two years. According to the council, less than a year after the policy was adopted the number of vacant homes fell by 34 percent.

A similar policy is being proposed for Melbourne, Australia, where Prosper Australia's 2015 speculative vacancies report showed that almost 5 percent of the city's total housing stock was vacant. The Camden Council noted that, while the rate hike was effective in reducing vacant homes, it is no panacea. Keeping housing affordable is a complex problem and there is no single, simple solution.

VIEW THE FULL POLICY

- camden.gov.uk/ccm/content/council-and-democracy/council-tax/discounts-and-exemptions/unoccupied-properties---changes-to-discount

City-owned Social Housing

Vienna, Austria

By Nikolas Kichler

Facing severe housing shortages in the early 20th century, Vienna has worked hard to address the issues of homelessness and affordability with what has become a hundred-year history of progressive housing policies. Beginning with the Tenancy Act in 1917 and followed by the community-driven housing cooperatives in the early 1920s, the subsequent "Red Vienna" period – 1924 to 1933 – and post World War II reforms, the city has continually made housing for all its residents a top priority.

Vienna's emphasis on affordable housing is evident in some of the policies that the city has implemented. For example, the city gives nonprofit cooperatives tax benefits as long as they invest profits back into housing, provides financial support for new construction, and caps the maximum rent that private owners can charge. The city also offers a free housing arbitration office and subsidies to low-income households.

The city currently owns and manages roughly 220,000 apartments, and is also home to a further 136,000 subsidized residences by nonprofit cooperatives. These co-ops originated during the reconstruction effort following WWII, and today are increasingly being initiated by "Baugruppen" (self-organized intentional housing groups). Examples of cooperative housing initiatives are the Sargfabrik, in 1996, or the Wohnprojekt Wien, in 2013. These housing cooperatives, combined with state-owned apartments, make up an incredible 60 percent of today's Viennese housing.

VIEW THE FULL POLICIES

- (German) www.ris.bka.gv.at/GeltendeFassung. wxe?Abfrage=Bundesnormen&Gesetzesnummer=10011509

- (German) www.wien.gv.at/recht/landesrecht-wien/rechtsvorschriften/html/b6300000.htm

- (German) www.jusline.at/Mietrechtsgesetz_(MRG)_Langversion.html

- (German) www.wien.gv.at/wohnen/schlichtungsstelle/index.html

- (German) www.wien.gv.at/wohnen/wohnbaufoerderung/wohnbeihilfe/index.html

Cooperative Housing

⚲ Multiple Locations, Egypt

By Sharon Ede

Egypt is a highly urbanized country, whose population is growing by 1.3 million people per year. Rapid urbanization has brought with it a lot of informal housing, squatting and slums.

Cooperative housing, which first emerged in Egypt in the 1930s, provides an affordable housing option for a large number of citizens. It was originally the domain of private developers until the 1950s, when the government became much more strongly involved in cooperative housing provision. Then, in the 1970s, private developers once again played a key role, with the state supporting cooperative housing development through loans to cooperative associations.

The status of housing co-ops in Egypt is such that there are provisions in the nation's constitution requiring the state to take care of cooperative associations. They are exempt from a range of taxes and fees under the country's legislation, which also requires the state to facilitate loans and offer discounts on land. Housing cooperatives receive a guaranteed discount of 25 percent on land owned by the government, which ministerial approval can bring up to as much as 50 percent.

About one-third of the 80 million strong Egyptian population are members of housing cooperatives. In the last 60 years, more than 2,300 housing co-op societies, comprising half a million dwellings, have been established.

VIEW THE FULL POLICY

• www.housinginternational.coop/co-ops/egypt

Legalization of Accessory Dwelling Units

◦ San Francisco, California, U.S.

By Nikolas Kichler

According to a report by the nonprofit SPUR, an Accessory Dwelling Unit (ADU) is an affordable "additional, self-contained dwelling unit located within the same lot as an existing residential building," such as do-it-yourself (DIY) "WikiHouses" or "Tiny Houses" in backyards. As many as 50,000 ADUs are estimated to have been built illegally over the years. The practice has historically been ignored by the city until recently, when they started removing roughly one hundred per year, partly due to neighbors' complaints. In many cases, this has been a cause of hardship for vulnerable families facing eviction.

To create a path for the legalization of the existing structures and to support the future construction of additional ADUs, the city has passed two key ordinances. Ordinance no. 43-14 offers a way for "granting legal status to existing dwelling units constructed without required permits." These units will now be covered by the city's rent-control ordinance. Ordinance no. 25-14 is a pilot program in District 8 that allows the demolition and reconstruction of existing accessory dwellings under certain conditions.

These policies will protect both property owners and renters, while encouraging urban infill in one of the most competitive housing markets in the United States.

VIEW THE FULL POLICIES

- Ordinance no. 25-14:
  www.sfbos.org/ftp/uploadedfiles/bdsupvrs/ordinances14/o0025-14.pdf

- Ordinance no. 43-14:
  www.sfbos.org/ftp/uploadedfiles/bdsupvrs/ordinances14/o0043-14.pdf

"

YOU ARE NEVER STRONG ENOUGH THAT YOU DON'T NEED HELP.

– CÉSAR CHÁVEZ

2

MOBILITY

Mobility is an intrinsic part of a city's ecosystem. However, many cities fail to provide comprehensive transport networks for their inhabitants. A major cause of this struggle is the privatization many cities have been subject to through allowing the terms of private companies to dictate transport, as well as the widespread prioritization of vehicles. And in an era of toxic production methods, irreversible climate change, and increasingly evident drawbacks of urban sprawl – such as traffic congestion and poor air quality – mobility policies should be seeking to reduce car dependency as much as possible.

Moreover, the urban mobility revolution has been dominated by transport network companies (TNCs) that utilize mobile apps or websites to pair drivers with passengers. They have largely emerged without holistic thinking about how they integrate with other public services and meet the mobility needs of cities as a whole. For a kind of infrastructure that requires so much public coordination and physical resources, the issue comes down to who owns and controls the services, and how they are incentivized to supply access to the public.

This chapter showcases a series of city policies where municipalities enable better access to mobility and incentivize cleaner transportation options through regulation. For-profit and non-profit organizations are also implementing their own solutions, which make use of existing transportation infrastructure or create new services entirely, all aimed toward increased public mobility. In both cases, we are seeing the emergence of more cooperatively- or city-owned and operated services that are equivalent to private TNCs. The great benefit of these publicly-oriented enterprise models is that they ensure that the value generated from the service transactions – such as from tolls, tickets, or passes – remains in the city where it was created and is reinvested into maintaining or expanding the infrastructure.

While digital technology has revolutionized privatized transportation, particularly through mobile on-demand ride-hailing services such as Uber and Lyft, cities are also making use of it in innovative ways to unleash the potential of underutilized public transport services. In particular, the "mobility as a service" approach is catching on. It is where modes of transport are integrated through a digital platform, and citizens choose a plan (similar to a phone plan) in which they can tailor their mobility needs.

In some ways, cities are the original sharing platform, having had emerged in part to facilitate access and exchange of all kinds: work, education, leisure, recreation, and more. That's why mobility within and beyond its borders is a critical feature of a functioning city. No matter how many services or opportunities are available in the city, they amount to nothing if people are not able to readily and affordably access them. In this sense, mobility is not an end in itself, but rather a means to an end. It is the glue that binds a city into a self-sustaining whole.

Sharon Ede

SafeMotos:
Shared, Safer Motorbike Taxis

◦ Kigali, Rwanda

By Sharon Ede

PROBLEM

In 2013, the World Health Organization estimated that 3,783 people had died in Rwanda due to road accidents. Although not always safe, "Mototaxis," or motorbike taxis, offered cost-effective transportation for low-income people and provided a livelihood for drivers. The challenge was to find a way to ensure the safety of passengers and create jobs for mototaxi drivers.

SOLUTION

SafeMotos is a digital platform that connects passengers with mototaxi drivers in Kigali, Rwanda. It incentivizes shared transportation by making it safer: Drivers are equipped with smartphones to monitor how safely they drive, by capturing and analyzing data on speed, acceleration, and location. SafeMotos drivers display distinctive red flags, which identifies them as safe drivers, and gives them a competitive edge in a crowded market.

Privately funded, and initiated by two locals who were themselves involved in a mototaxi accident, SafeMotos is not just an app: It's an initiative to help change the culture of driving in Kigali, and other African cities, with plans to ensure SafeMotos drivers are all trained in basic first aid.

"The authorities are often ambivalent towards [moto] drivers because they associate them with crime and disorder... They are trying to show they are legitimate people just trying to make an income."

Peter Kariuki, co-founder of SafeMotos

Source: The Guardian

SafeMotos' model, which also helps reduce carbon emissions and traffic congestion, can be adopted in cities around the world.

RESULTS

- By late 2015, 42 drivers had signed up and 3,000 trips had been completed using SafeMotos, with plenty of scope for the expansion of the system, as there are an estimated 10,000 mototaxi drivers in Kigali, according to co-founder Barrett Nash, in a piece published on ICTWorks.org.

- As reported by Huck Magazine, information about driver behaviour gathered by the SafeMotos app is combined with passenger ratings to determine a "safety score," and drivers must achieve at least a 90 percent rating.

RESOURCES

- SafeMotos: www.safemotos.com

- The Guardian article: www.theguardian.com/global-development/2015/dec/28/safemotos-rwanda-motorbike-taxis-road-safety

- ICTWorks.org article: www.ictworks.org/2015/12/30/using-smartphones-to-fight-africas-second-greatest-killer

COOP Taxi:
Giving the Power Back to Driver

▽ Seoul, South Korea

By Leila Collins

PROBLEM

The taxi industry in Seoul has exploited drivers for some time. Indeed, in order to drive a taxi in South Korea, drivers are required to pay 120,000 won (approximately $105) in daily fees. This situation has been further exacerbated by the introduction of the KakaoTaxi app. Launched March 31, 2015, KakaoTaxi is a platform that connects drivers to passengers directly. While increasing efficiency, the introduction of KakaoTaxi has also accelerated competition, forcing drivers to lower prices significantly. However, downward financial pressure on taxi drivers has forced them to seek out passengers who are more financially lucrative. This has been a significant challenge to both the taxi drivers who are struggling to make a living and to passengers who are in need of basic transportation services.

SOLUTION

In response to this challenge, former lawmaker Park Gye Dong, chairperson of COOP Taxi, developed a system to give drivers an alternative to the exploitation of taxi companies. The system brought together 184 drivers who invested 4 billion won ($3.3 million total). Each driver invests at least 25 million won ($21,413) to become a

"I believe our cooperative has practically shown how humans can control capital, not the other way around."

Park Kye-dong, Korea COOP chairperson

Source: Korea Herald

member of the cooperative, and then receives a dividend proportionate to the initial investment on top of regular earnings. Unlike traditional taxi companies, drivers do not have to pay any daily fees to the cooperative. The unique value of COOP is that it allows drivers to be owners of the system itself.

RESULTS
- Drivers now enjoy better pay and working conditions. For instance, they only need to work five days a week instead of the industry standard of six.

RESOURCES
- COOP (Korean): coop-taxi.kr/

- Pulse News article: pulsenews.co.kr/view.php?year=2015&no=760294

- Korea Times article: www.koreatimes.co.kr/www/common/printpreview. asp?categoryCode=197&newsIdx=184928

Walking School Bus:
Shared Journeys to School

♡ Worldwide

By Sharon Ede

PROBLEM

Fears for children's safety during their commute to school means fewer students are riding bikes or walking to school. More students are being driven to school, which results in more traffic, further eroding students' ability to make their way to school safely. This also contributes to traffic congestion, increased stress on parents and guardians, and lost opportunities for physical activity for students.

SOLUTION

Conceived by Australian creative planner and urbanist David Engwicht in 1992, the Walking School Bus is an agreed, set route to and from school supervised by adult volunteer "drivers" (often parents) who collect students from various stops. The bus is free, and every child is welcome, whether or not they have a parent who can be a driver.

The Walking School Bus can be as simple and low cost, or as elaborate, as the students and drivers wish to make it. A ratio of one adult to eight students is recommended. Benefits to students include learning to negotiate the road and their neighborhood, improving social interaction, and getting physical exercise. Benefits

Auckland Mayor Phil Goff

Source: city of Auckland news brief

to parents include reducing fuel costs, saving time, and gaining peace of mind in knowing that their children are going to school safely. The Walking School Bus often has the support of a local authority and/or the school, but can be self-organized and run by parents and students. The Bicycle Train is a version of the Walking School Bus where the mode of transport is cycling.

RESULTS

- The Walking School Bus has become a global phenomenon, widely adopted in the U.K. and other parts of Europe, Australia, New Zealand, and the U.S.

- By 2010, Western Australia had established 39 active Walking School Bus routes at 26 primary schools. Routes are approximately 1 km, and surveys revealed that there were more than 10,000 "trips" made in the first three terms of the year. During the same period, these efforts saved nearly 3.5 tons of greenhouse gas emissions.

- Auckland has over 350 active walking school buses, with more than 4,000 children walking to school.

- A 2011 study published in the journal *Pediatrics* revealed that children who were randomly chosen to participate in a Walking School Bus over a five-week period in Houston, Texas, increased their weekly rate of active commuting by an average of 38 percent.

RESOURCES

- "The Walking School Bus: A Guide for Parents and Teachers": www.travelsmart.gov.au/schools/pubs/guide.pdf

- "Simple Guide to Starting a Walking School Bus": www.walkingschoolbus.org

Multimodal Toolkit:
Bundle of Subsidized Discounts for Transportation

⚲ Denver and Boulder, Colorado, U.S.

———

By Sharon Ede

Low-income households require affordable and accessible transport options, but many cities simply don't have enough public transport alternatives to meet the need. With grants from the Denver and Boulder city governments and other partners, the nonprofit organization CarShare created the Multimodal Toolkit. It offers highly subsidized transit passes, discounts to use the cities' car-sharing program, and free or discounted bike sharing memberships. The toolkit was also a way to engage residents with available modes of transportation in the area, as well as providing firsthhand education on them, such as by showing where shared cars are stationed and providing bike safety trainings. The program ran from spring 2014 to February 2016, during which time an initial survey showed that three quarters of recipients used at least one of the offerings from the toolkit.

RESOURCES

- Multimodal Toolkit: carshare.org/affordable-housing-multi-modal-toolkit

- Mobility Lab article: mobilitylab.org/2014/12/22/boulder-makes-it-easy-for-low-income-residents-to-take-bus-bike-and-carshare/

Whim:

Platform for Both Public and Private Transportation Options

Helsinki, Finland

―――

By Sharon Ede

In many cities, there are separate ticketing systems across several public transport options. And when payments are disjointed, mobility can be highly inefficient and inconvenient. To make transportation as easy as purchasing a mobile phone service, a startup in Helsinki, Finland, launched the world's first mobility-as-a-service (MaaS) platform. It's called Whim, and it uses mobile technology to coordinate a range of public and private modes of transport, enabling access to cars, taxis, buses, trains, and bike shares. The app handles ticketing and payments, and helps people find the best route to where they need to go, when they need to go. Whim offers monthly packages as well as pay-as-you-go options. Launched in mid-June 2016 by MaaS Global in Helsinki, Whim already has plans to expand the platform to other cities.

RESOURCES

- Whim: maas.global

- MaaS Global article: maas.global/whim-the-worlds-first-all-inclusive-mobility-service-promises-to-change-urban-travel-forever/

RideAustin:
A Local Nonprofit Ride-hailing Enterprise

Austin, Texas, U.S.

By Leila Collins

The rapid proliferation of ride-sharing applications like Uber and Lyft leave both drivers and riders at risk from worker exploitation and personal harm from unvetted drivers, respectively. Many cities have not had a chance to catch up and regulate the platforms to protect their residents, but some have started doing so, not without consequences. In 2016, Uber and Lyft pulled their operations from Austin, Texas, out of protest after the city council passed an ordinance requiring ride-hailing companies to do fingerprint-based criminal background checks among other things. Since they left, however, new ride-sharing alternatives began to thrive there. The most notable one being RideAustin, a local nonprofit ride-hailing organization whose objective is to pay its drivers well and keep costs low for riders. Their mobile app has a feature that enables customers to round their fare up to the nearest dollar, then the difference is donated to a local charity of their choice. As of March 2017, the service had given over $100,000 to Austin-based groups through this program. RideAustin saw exponential growth in ridership within the first year of its launch, reaching its millionth ride in eight months. In May 2017, the state of Texas passed a law backed by Uber and Lyft that pre-empts Austin's local ordinance. Now Uber and Lyft have returned to Austin on their terms, which has hurt RideAustin's business. It remains to be seen if RideAustin can stand up to Uber and Lyft's artificially low, venture capital subsidized rates and marketing power.

RESOURCES

- RideAustin: www.rideaustin.com

- Austin Ordinance No. 20151217-075:
  www.austintexas.gov/edims/document.cfm%3Fid=245769

- MIT Technology Review on Austin's ride-hailing situation: www.technologyreview.com/s/603792/hailing-a-different-ride-in-austin/?set=603799

"

WE HAVE WHAT WE NEED, IF WE USE WHAT WE HAVE.

– EDGAR CAHN

San Francisco Prioritizes Parking for Car Sharing

San Francisco, California, U.S.

By Sharon Ede

Carsharing provides many social, economic, and environmental benefits, such as reduced household costs, increased access to transportation for lower-income households, less traffic congestion, and lower levels of greenhouse gas emissions. However, existing urban transportation systems do not always offer "affirmative action" for shared mobility, especially in cities where competition for space is at a premium.

Designating parking spaces exclusively for shared cars offers physical infrastructure as well as visible support for shared mobility. More importantly, it encourages more car sharing by offering a more convenient and cost-effective service for users.

In 2010, the city of San Francisco amended its planning code to incentivize car sharing by incorporating two new development approval requirements:

- Newly constructed buildings incorporating residential uses or existing buildings being converted to residential use must provide a certain number of permanent car-share parking spaces depending on expected numbers of residences.
- Specific nonresidential developments must also dedicate a percentage of their parking spaces to "short-term, transient use by vehicles from certified carsharing organizations" or similar programs.

Subsequently, and as reported by a 2014 SFGate article, the San Francisco Municipal Transportation Agency (SFMTA) announced in 2014 that 900 of 281,000 on-street spaces would be set aside for use by customers of car-sharing firms Zipcar, City CarShare (a local nonprofit now merged with Getaround), and Getaround (a leader in peer-to-peer car sharing). The policy ensures that spaces are located in all socioeconomic areas by requiring that at least 30 percent of spaces are in the city's periphery and by offering lower prices for those spots.

The SFTMA's January 2017 carsharing parking pilot evaluation report found that "placing carshare spaces on-street increases shared vehicle access, convenience, and visibility." As a result of participating in car sharing, 17 percent of members who owned a car reported selling or donating one. In addition, on-street car-share vehicles were used dramatically more (six hours per day versus one) and by more people (19 versus two per month) than private vehicles. Also, the data "showed that 80 percent of the on-street carshare spaces were shared between more than 10 people monthly."

These policy measures highlight important challenges and opportunities. For instance, city support of car sharing through designated off-street parking must be communicated carefully. Though only a small percentage of on-street spots were made available to car-sharing organizations – and they pay the city for spaces – a 2014 Streetsblog article noted that the policy created a perception among some residents that public space was being gifted to private companies. The public benefits of car sharing – and how it can be supported by designating spaces – is an important communication challenge, especially in cities where parking spaces are scarce. In addition, the off-street parking ordinance per-mits only round-trip car-sharing organizations to use designated spaces, not one-way car-sharing services like Car2Go, where vehicles can be left anywhere and not just at the point of origin. Policymakers should consider supporting all modes of car sharing, including one-way options.

VIEW THE FULL POLICY
- www.sfbos.org/ftp/uploadedfiles/bdsupvrs/ordinances10/o0286-10.pdf

RESOURCES
- San Francisco's car-sharing requirements and guidelines, including its car-share organization certification process: sf-planning.org/car-share-requirements-and-guidelines

- SFMTA's 2017 car-sharing parking pilot evaluation report: www.sfmta.com/sites/default/files/projects/2017/Carshare_eval_final.pdf

Ride-sharing Companies Charged Mileage Fees to Help Fund Infrastructure

♀ Sao Paulo, Brazil

By Sharon Ede

Around 19 million people live in the Sao Paulo metropolitan area. Traffic congestion is so severe that on-demand helicopter hailing between airports, hotels and convention centers has commenced operation in the city, according to a June 2016 Sydney Morning Herald news report.

A July 2014 story in The City Fix reported that the lost work hours and wasted fuel due to congestion cost the cities of Rio de Janiero and Sao Paulo around 140.4 billion reais ($43 billion) in 2013, or about 8 percent of each city's GDP. While ride-sharing is one way to address congestion, transportation network companies (TNCs) are not contributing to the cost of the public infrastructure they rely on to generate revenue.

In May 2016, the Mayor of Sao Paulo, South America's largest city, announced that TNCs – commercial entities who match drivers with passengers via an app or web platform – could operate in the city in exchange for prepaid fees that will average of 0.10 reais ($0.03) per vehicle/kilometer traveled (the regulation exempts free ride-sharing services). This approach means TNCs would contribute revenue on a pay-as-you-drive basis to help the city maintain the road network and other public infrastructure.

The policy is still new, so an evaluation is not yet available. However, the city anticipates that the new regulation will raise 37.5 million reais ($11.5 million) per year. The decree requires TNCs to share their data (origin and destination, distances traveled, price, etc.), which will enable the city to better analyze, plan, and manage the city's transportation network, including the ability to incentivize TNCs to complement public transit, limit their contribution to rush hour congestion, and better serve low-income travelers and disabled persons.

VIEW THE FULL POLICY

- (Portuguese) www.legisweb.com.br/legislacao/?id=320363

RESOURCES

- News report of the approved plan:
  www.reuters.com/article/us-uber-tech-brazil-idUSKCN0Y12TL

- A summary of the proposal (not the approved policy, but this follows closely to what was approved): blogs.worldbank.org/transport/sao-paulo-s-innovative-proposal-regulate-shared-mobility-pricing-vehicle-use

Bike Sharing for All

Portland, Oregon, U.S.

By Leila Collins

Biking has become a way of life in Portland and many other cities around the world. Riders enjoy reduced transit costs, health benefits, and social opportunities. In most cities, however, these benefits are only accessible for those who can ride traditional bikes, or the physically disabled who can afford special bikes. In Portland, riders lobbied the city government to think about disabled riders in designing a bike-sharing system.

The city will eventually offer adaptive bikes for the physically disabled as part of the 1,000-bike and 100-station bike sharing system that launched in July 2016. The city first conducted a series of interviews with disabled riders to understand their needs. They found that, in addition to needing a variety of adaptive bikes, disabled riders often required storage options for wheelchairs and assistance at bike share stations. Adaptive bikes are designed to fit the needs of individual riders. Some are designed with three wheels to accommodate riders who have trouble balancing. Others are heavy duty to accommodate larger riders or offer hand pedals for riders with limited or no lower body mobility. During the interviews, officials discovered that disabled riders were looking to ride for exercise and recreation, so it is crucial to offer more adaptive bikes and services near trails, rather than at commuter bike stations.

The adaptive bike program was scheduled to roll out in June, 2017. The city is holding or has held educational events, such as the adaptive bike clinic, and providing scholarships for biking classes, to ensure more people can enjoy the benefits of the forthcoming bike-sharing facilities.

RESOURCES
- Adaptive Bicycle Rental Pilot Project:
  www.portlandoregon.gov/transportation/73371

- News story covering the policy:
  sharedusemobilitycenter.org/news/can-bikesharing-serve-disabled-riders

- More on the adaptive bicycling pilot project from the city of Portland:
  www.portlandoregon.gov/transportation/article/582518

Municipal Car Sharing
Sydney, Australia

By Sharon Ede

Australia's culture of car dependency is creating unnecessary urban congestion, time and financial costs for households and business, and contributing
to Australia's high level of carbon emissions. The city of Sydney introduced a
car-sharing policy in 2011 to encourage shared use of vehicles.

Car-sharing operators must offer fuel-efficient and low-emissions vehicles,
make the cars available via a 24-hour web- and phone-based booking system,
and provide a monthly report on the use of car-sharing parking spaces. The
policy contains provisions that prevent spaces allocated to car sharing from
being sold or transferred to new operators, and there is an annual fee for
car-sharing operators to cover the administration costs of the policy.

According to the city of Sydney, they currently provide around 700 car-sharing
spaces, which are utilized by two operators. As reported by Sydney Media,
just five years after the policy was introduced the city has already exceeded its
target of signing up 10 percent of households by 2016. Moreover, an average of
nine people sign up to the scheme every day, which is utilized by over 26,000
customers – roughly 19,000 residents and 7,000 local businesses. An independent evaluation of the policy's impact was commissioned by the city in 2012.
The SGS Economics and Planning study found that car sharing had already
saved users $21 million per year, mostly from deferred car purchases amount-
ing to $18.5 million. The policy also contributed to decreased travel times,
reduced congestion, and lower carbon emissions.

VIEW THE FULL POLICY
- www.cityofsydney.nsw.gov.au/__data/assets/pdf_file/0010/109099/2016-
  631840-Car-Sharing-Policy-2016-accessible.pdf

RESOURCES
- City of Sydney car-sharing website:
  www.cityofsydney.nsw.gov.au/live/residents/car-sharing

Comprehensive Shared Mobility Strategy

Milan, Italy

By Sharon Ede

Milan has one of the highest rates of car ownership in Europe, with over 51 cars for every 100 inhabitants (London is 30:100), and consequently the city faces urban congestion challenges. To address this issue, Milan has implemented one of the most comprehensive mobility plans in the world.

Milan introduced bike sharing in 2008, adding 1,000 electric bikes to its fleet in 2014, followed by a scooter-sharing scheme in 2015. In 2013, the city called for expressions of interest from car-sharing service operators, and three providers now offer almost 2,000 shared cars, including 100 electric cars.

The car-sharing program gained 50,000 users in a matter of weeks and, in the first year, reduced the number of private cars on the road by 13,000. There are currently over 200,000 subscribers to the car-sharing schemes, and 37,000 subscribers to the bike-sharing program. A congestion charge has also reduced traffic congestion by 28 percent, and generated 2 million euros ($2.2 million) per year in revenue for the city to continue to invest in shared-mobility infrastructure. Milan's comprehensive mobility program is being evaluated for implementation by several other Italian and European cities.

VIEW THE FULL POLICY
- nws.eurocities.eu/MediaShell/media/CitiesInAction_MilanSharingMobility_Nov15.pdf

RESOURCES
- Car-sharing development strategy in Milan (report):
  transport.mos.ru/common/upload/docs/1443535035_ValentinoSevino.pdf

Enabling Carpooling with Emergency Ride Support

Minneapolis, Minnesota, U.S.

By Leila Collins

Increased carpooling and use of public transit reduces the number of drivers on the road, alleviating congestion and cutting down on carbon emissions and smog. Still, many who are open to the idea of carpooling or using public transit prefer to rely on the flexibility of a private car, in the event they have an emergency or need to stay at work late, for example.

Officials in Minneapolis eliminated this concern to encourage alternatives to driving alone by instituting a Guaranteed Ride Home (GRH) program (also known as emergency ride home). Anyone who commutes to work or school at least three times a week by riding the train, bus, carpool/vanpool, bicycle, or walking is eligible to participate. This innovative city-sponsored commuter insurance covers the cost of a taxi, ride share, or rental car up to $100 a year (or four annual rides) in the event of an emergency or an overtime shift which makes it impossible to use normal transportation. This program carries extra significance for workers and students without driver's licenses, the elderly, those who cannot afford a car, and those with disabilities that prevent them from driving.

Minneapolis is just one of many cities in the United States to implement this easily replicable policy.

VIEW THE FULL POLICY
• www.metrotransit.org/guaranteed-ride-home

RESOURCES
• Emergency Ride Home Toolkit: www.bestworkplaces.org/erhkit

FOOD

If a city manages to provide all its residents with fresh, local, and healthy food, then that city has leapfrogged toward an inclusive and equitable society: such is the level of importance of food in a city. Food not only forms an integral part of human activity, but also of the economy.

What is the role of cities and citizens in creating a resilient food system?

There is a greater interest in creating more resilient cities where residents produce what they need, in order to minimize waste and dependency on industrial-scale food production and retailing. This, combined with individual interest to learn and reconnect with the food system, has given rise to a number of urban and community gardens. This bottom-up movement of urban agriculture is also seeking a structural support by policy makers. Several grassroot communities around the world are finding innovative ways to distribute the surplus food grown or cooked which otherwise would go to waste. For example, the League of Urban Canners, in Boston, have developed a cooperative infrastructure to map, harvest, preserve, and share tons of otherwise wasted fruit by making agreements with property owners and sharing the work of fruit harvesting and preserving. FoodCloud, in Ireland, has developed an app that allows charities to collect surplus fresh food directly from retailers, using smart technology. This food is then distributed to people in need.

The case studies and policies in the chapter illuminate the relationship between cities and food. They demonstrate a new model of food production, acquisition, and consumption that is led by citizens through bottom-up innovations and top-down sustainable engagements.

Khushboo Balwani

FoodCloud:

Linking up Businesses and Charities to Redistribute Surplus Food to People in Need

◊ Dublin, Ireland

By Anna Davies *(SHARECITY and Trinity College Dublin)*

PROBLEM

Globally, around one-third of all food that is produced is wasted, according to the Food and Agriculture Organization of the United Nations. Large quantities of this food waste are fit for human consumption, but become surplus due to packaging damage, short shelf-life, or qualities that are considered "imperfect." So how can we improve food security and sustainability of food systems?

SOLUTION

Having identified the mismatch between organizations with surplus food and organizations that provide for people experiencing food poverty, FoodCloud developed a "smart-simple" app to facilitate a mutually beneficial exchange of food that can be scaled. Using a custom-built technology platform, participating businesses post details of their surplus food and identify a time period for its collection. This posting triggers an automated text message to participating charities in the area that can indicate that they would like to pick up the food. Recognizing the challenges that charities face in picking up food late at night – the time when businesses often

"We were an early partner with FoodCloud and Tesco, and the difference it has made to our residents is terrific! The food brings the women who live with us together and we've seen strong friendships develop as they swap and share food and recipes."

Orla Gilroy, CEO of Daisyhouse Housing Association

Source: FoodCloud

identify their surplus food – FoodCloud has also introduced a food rescue team of volunteers in Dublin, Ireland, who use a donated electric vehicle to facilitate pickup and drop-offs between businesses and charities.

RESULTS

- FoodCloud has distributed over 20 million meals in England and Ireland diverting over 9,000 tons of potential food waste from landfills.

- FoodCloud works with over 5,500 food industry and community partners.

- FoodCloud also offers opportunities for community capacity building through volunteering and other means.

RESOURCES

- FoodCloud: food.cloud

Seva Cafe Volunteers preparing the food for the day. Photographer: Tharanath Gajendra. Source: Sent by photographer. Usage rights: licensed under CC BY 4.0

Seva Cafe:
A Pay-it-Forward Experiment in Peer-to-Peer Generosity
⚲ Ahmedabad, India

By Khushboo Balwani

PROBLEM

Food – the most basic necessity of life – is becoming scarce. Approximately 795 million people in the world don't have access to sufficient food to be healthy, according to the World Food Program. But what if we turned that assumption of scarcity into abundance and started sharing generously with strangers? Seva Cafe might not solve the problem of food scarcity, but it is a promising step in the right direction.

SOLUTION

Seva Cafe launched in 2006 in Ahmedabad, India, as an experiment in peer-to-peer generosity and the family model of sharing food. The whole organization is run on a daily basis by seven to eight volunteers who make and serve meals to guests. Based on the model of gift economy, the meals are served as an unconditional gift, with no price. Guests may choose to pay or volunteer with the organization, but they aren't required to do either.

The bill at Seva cafe reads "0/-" with only this footnote, "Your meal was a gift from someone who came before you. To keep the chain of gifts alive, we invite you to pay it forward for those who dine after you." The entire financial process and op-

"I think when you come into a space with strangers and you feel at home, you suddenly realise that this world is one family."

Anjali Desai, volunteer at Seva Cafe

eration is completely transparent and run by the energy of giving. Seva Cafe is also famously known as "Karma Kitchen" in many countries. It is part of a larger trend of pay-it-forward restaurants.

RESULTS

- Seva Cafe operates seven days a week and serves around 60 guests daily.

- Customers and volunteers are empowered by exercising their generosity.

RESOURCES

- Moved by Love: www.movedbylove.org/projects/sevacafe

- Freegan Pony, Paris: www.facebook.com/Freegan-Pony-1627473020835867

- Selma Cafe, Ann Arbor: selmacafe.org/about

Incredible Edible Todmorden:
Access to Local Food for All

◉ Todmorden, U.K.

By Khushboo Balwani

PROBLEM

The rapid expansion of cities is breaking the relationship that people have with the food ecosystem. Although the problem is receiving attention by some city officials, and they are adopting new sustainability programs and policies, it is a time-consuming, top-down process with an uncertain impact. What if there was a bottom-up, citizens-driven way to achieve impact? Cities are centers of enormous human resources. Incredible Edible Todmorden shows it is possible to create a more sustainable and affordable food systems by leveraging connections with friends, families, neighbors, and local community groups.

SOLUTION

Back in 2007, a woman in a small town called Todmorden, in the northern part of England, dug up her prized rose garden. She planted vegetables, knocked down the garden wall, and put up a sign saying, "Help Yourself."

This small action grew into a movement that has transformed Todmorden into a town in which citizens are reshaping their surroundings. The Incredible Edible Todmorden movement has turned all the public spaces, from the front yard of a police

"We're starting to build resilience ourselves. We're starting to reinvent community ourselves, and we've done it all without a flipping strategy document."

Pam Warhurst, co-founder of Incredible Edible Todmorden

Source: TED Talk

station to railway stations, into farms filled with edible herbs and vegetables. Locals and tourists pluck fruits and vegetables for free.

This novel idea, which is also called "open-source food," promises a future with food for all. The project shares a participatory vision of "three plates" – community, education, and business. Schools grow food, businesses donate goods and services, and shops sell planter boxes.

RESULTS

- As a result of the huge success of the project, the Incredible Edible Network was set up in 2012 to attract grant funding and support the replication of the project globally. There are now 100 Incredible Edible groups across the U.K. More are popping up all the time around the globe.

- The initiative has opened up new opportunities for local farmers and tourism.

- The movement has also fostered a sense of community and responsibility among the local residents, interaction and bonding among the neighbors, and connections with spaces like police stations, cemeteries, and prisons.

RESOURCES

- Incredible Edible network: incredibleediblenetwork.org.uk

- Incredible Edible Todmorden: www.incredible-edible-todmorden.co.uk

- Shareable article:
  www.shareable.net/blog/10-steps-toward-an-incredible-edible-town

League of Urban Canners:
Stewarding Urban Orchards

◊ Boston, Massachusetts, U.S.

By Oona Morrow *(SHARECITY and Trinity College Dublin)*

Planting an urban fruit tree is more than a lifetime commitment – it is an intergenerational civic responsibility. Each summer, in Greater Boston, a huge amount of backyard fruit falls to the ground and sidewalk, where it rots and creates a mess. Property owners and municipalities are often pressured to remove these "nuisances," while many urban residents are struggling to access local and organic food sources. The League of Urban Canners has developed a network of individuals to map, harvest, preserve, and share this otherwise wasted fruit. They make agreements with property owners to share the work of fruit harvesting and preserving, as well as tree and arbor pruning. The preserved fruits are shared between property owners (10 percent), preservers (70 percent), and harvesters (20 percent). Each season the completely volunteer-run enterprise harvests and preserves about 5,000 pounds of fruit from a database of more than 300 trees and arbors. Myriad acts of cooperation sustain this urban commons, in which harvesters, property owners, preservers, and eaters learn to share responsibility, resources, and care for each other and their urban environment.

RESOURCES
• League of Urban Canners: www.leagueofurbancanners.org

Restaurant Day ('Ravintolapäivä'):
Fostering Cross-cultural Gatherings Through Shared Meals

📍 Helsinki, Finland

By Khushboo Balwani

In big cities, people of many different cultures live in close proximity. However, there often aren't enough chances for them to intermingle and experience the diverse traditions within their city. In an effort to bring people together and foster cross-cultural interaction, local organizers in Helsinki, Finland, created "Ravintolapäivä," or Restaurant Day. Initiated in 2011, it began as a food carnival where anyone with a passion for food was encouraged to run a "restaurant" in their private home or in public spaces for a single day. Even though the pop-up restaurants charge money for the meals, the emphasis is not on profit, but rather on community teamwork and cultural exchange. During the event, Helsinki is transformed by hundreds of these informal restaurants serving a wide range of cuisines in this city-wide street festival. The event is put on through distributed organization – individual volunteer restaurateurs are responsible for finding a location, managing the menu and invitations, and setting the meal prices. Now, Restaurant Day has become a global movement, with over 27,000 pop-up restaurants having served over 3 million community members across 75 countries.

RESOURCES
• Ravintolapäivä: www.restaurantday.org/en

Kitchen Share:
A Sustainable Community Resource for Home Cooks

◉ Portland, Oregon, U.S.

––––

By Marion Weymes *(SHARECITY and Trinity College Dublin)*

Kitchen appliances can be superfluous uses of money and cupboard space, especially for city residents with tight budgets and small homes. Yet interest in healthy eating is growing. More people are trying out unusual food preparation techniques, which can require unique appliances. Kitchen Share, launched in 2012, is a kitchen tool-lending library for home cooks in Portland, Oregon. It enables community members to borrow a wide variety of kitchen appliances such as dehydrators, mixers, and juicers. Members can check out over 400 items online using affordable lending library software from myTurn. With two locations in Portland, Kitchen Share helps residents save money, learn new skills from neighbors, and reduce their environmental footprint. As a nonprofit community resource for home cooks, Kitchen Share only asks for a one-time donation upon joining, providing affordable access to otherwise expensive and bulky items while building a more resource-efficient city.

RESOURCES

• Kitchen Share: kitchenshare.org

• Toolkit for starting a lending library: sharestarter.org/tools

• myTurn lending library software: myturn.com

"

THERE IS NO JOY IN POSSESSION WITHOUT SHARING.

– ERASMUS

Urban Agriculture Incentive Zone

♀ San Francisco, California, U.S.

By Khushboo Balwani

In cities across the world, urban agriculture is increasing access to local healthy food, connecting communities, and creating local jobs. On Aug. 7, 2014, San Francisco was the first city in California to establish an urban agriculture incentive zone (UAIZ), as permitted by state Assembly Bill 551, to address two large obstacles faced by farmers and gardeners – access to land and secure land tenure. This act allows owners of vacant property within San Francisco to apply for tax reduction in exchange for putting their land into agricultural use for at least five years. The law includes a number of requirements that ensure community development and resource sharing. For example, in order to qualify for tax reductions, property owners must include in their urban farm or gardening plan some interface with the public, through either distribution or sales of food; educational activities such as classes and workshops; or that the site will be used as a community garden with members other than the property owner's family.

To ensure its best application, an agricultural commissioner is appointed to review the plan and to conduct annual inspections. Another interesting feature of the law is that it limits the use of pesticides and/or fertilizers to those that meet organic standards. San Francisco's Recreation and Park Departments is involved to help coordinate community outreach, education, and the application process. The UAIZ law makes healthy food more accessible, lessens landowners' tax burden, creates jobs, makes use of vacant lots thus reducing blight and crime, and in general helps regenerate communities.

VIEW THE FULL POLICY

- www.spur.org/sites/default/files/blog_post_pdfs/SF_AB551_Implementing_Leg_Board_Packet_July_22.pdf

RESOURCES

- Local news report about the law: www.sfgate.com/bayarea/article/S-F-property-owners-to-get-tax-break-from-5725876.php

- Implementation guide for Urban Agriculture Incentive Zones Act: ucanr.edu/sites/UrbanAg/files/190763.pdf

Resolution to Support Seed Saving and Sharing

⦿ Duluth, Minnesota, U.S.

—

By Neal Gorenflo

Seed saving and seed libraries are on the rise as communities deepen their commitment to healthy, delicious, local food. However, several U.S. states, including Minnesota and Pennsylvania, began applying regulation meant for commercial seed producers to small-scale, community seed libraries in 2014. Commercial regulations make it impossible for small seed libraries to operate because of the high cost of commercial seed labeling, testing and permitting. In reaction, the seed library community, the Sustainable Economies Law Center (SELC), and Shareable worked together to educate regulators and amend or enact new measures to allow seed saving and sharing. As a result, several U.S. cities and states including Duluth, Minnesota, passed new measures in December 2014.

VIEW THE FULL POLICY

- Duluth's seed saving and sharing resolution: duluth-mn.granicus.com/ MetaViewer.php?view_id=&clip_id=44&meta_id=9320

RESOURCES

- SELC's Seed Law Tool Shed: www.theselc.org/seed_law_resources

Agroecological Strategy to Increase Food Sovereignty

♀ Havana, Cuba

By Khushboo Balwani

Cuba entered a severe economic depression after the 1991 collapse of the Soviet Union, its primary trading partner at the time. As a result, imports plummeted by 80 percent. Food, oil, pesticide, fertilizer, and farm equipment imports were hit hard. This devastated Cuba's economy and industrial food system.

According to the book, "The Greening Revolution: Cuba's Experiment with Organic Agriculture," Cuba was forced to undergo "the largest conversion from conventional agriculture to organic or semi-organic farming that the world has ever known."

Havana, the capital of and largest city in Cuba, played a prominent role in addressing food shortages through urban agriculture policies and practices that dramatically increased the availability of fresh food in the city. The strategy focused on soil fertility, organic management, ecological pest control, the rational use of local resources, participatory plant breeding, increased land access, and farmer-to-farmer and farmer-to-researcher knowledge dissemination. It was a massive and largely successful effort. Here are a few key policies and programs:

- A right-to-farm policy and provision of agro-ecological inputs: According to a 2014 Guardian article, a large amount of unused state-owned farmland was made available to private farmers and cooperatives in 2008. In addition, and as reported by a 2009 Monthly Review article, "more than two hundred facilities provide needed input for urban agriculture – producing, providing, and/or selling seeds, organic fertilizers, biological pest control preparations, technical services, and advice."

- Promotion of agroecological technology through education and research: Universities and research centers were reoriented to make agroecology the dominant agricultural paradigm in Havana. This was supported by a rich inventory of agroecology science and practice.

- Fair prices for farmers and other incentives: Farmers and small-scale gardeners can sell their excess production at farmers' markets at a profit, as a result of government policy. This gives urban farmers financial incentives to grow, along with other incentives such as social recognition.

As a result of these efforts, Cuba's urban farms supply 70 percent or more of all the fresh vegetables consumed in cities such as Havana, and 350,000 related jobs were created between 1997 and 2009, as per Monthly Review articles from 2012 and 2009, respectively.

RESOURCES

- PBS minidocumentary on Cuba's urban agriculture:
  www.pbs.org/newshour/bb/cuba-can-teach-america-farming

- Academic study on the evolution of urban agriculture in Cuba:
  agrarianstudies.macmillan.yale.edu/sites/default/files/files/
  colloqpapers/01premat.pdf

Creating a Vibrant Local Food Ecosystem through Government-NGO Collaboration

♀ Loos-en-Gohelle, France

By Myriam Bouré *(OuiShare and Open Food Network Community)*

Up until a few years ago, the residents of Loos-en-Gohelle, a small town in rural northwestern France with over 6,000 residents, consumed imported industrial food products despite significant local production. In addition to the negative health impacts of their diet, this practice also hurt the local economy. In 2013, the town government of Loos-en-Gohelle started a project called VITAL as part of an ambitious program to improve the diets of Loos-en-Gohelle residents.

The project was built on an existing initiative called Anges Gardins, run by a local association that has worked on community gardens and food education for years. It is also part of a long-term, comprehensive transition to a diverse, sustainable local economy from one dependent on coal mining – an industry that vanished when the French government closed the region's coal mines in 1990, in favor of cheaper imports. Food is viewed as a cross-cutting issue, capable of supporting transition in other sectors.

The policy has a two-pronged strategy to meet the goal. First, to stimulate the demand for local, organic food through education, gardening ambassadors, free produce from open food gardens, and more. The town government led by example, by shifting to 100 percent organic food procurement for schools and 15 percent for retirement homes.

Second, to encourage farmers to convert to organic farming and support food distribution. To help achieve this, the town offered farmers free access to land on the condition that they grow organically and that they convert some of their own existing agricultural land to organic as well, thus raising the share of lands grown organically to 10 percent. Terre d'Opale, another local association, coordinates the farmers to ensure diversity of local production and manage distribution. Distribution is handled weekly through a combination of an online store, delivery of food boxes to local collection points, and procurement through catering businesses.

The program has operated successfully for three years. As the program benefits the entire local food ecosystem, including consumers, farmers, food kitchens, and distributors, it continues to grow and serve more and more of the community.

VIEW THE FULL POLICY

- (French) http://www.loos-en-gohelle.fr/wp-content/
uploads/2015/03/2014-07_VITAL.pdf

RESOURCES

- A report on the VITAL project (French): www.cerdd.org/layout/set/embed/
Parcours-thematiques/Alimentation-durable/Initiatives-du-parcours-5/Loos-
en-Gohelle-une-dynamique-d-alimentation-durable-qui-stimule-l-evolution-
des-pratiques

Community Food and Nutrition Security Through 'People's Restaurants'

♀ Belo Horizonte, Brazil

By Khushboo Balwani

Recognizing the need to make basic foods more readily available to low-income people, the "Restaurantes Populares" initiative (People's Restaurants, or Popular Restaurants in the original Portuguese) has been a key part of Belo Horizonte's pioneering Food and Nutrition Security Policy (Law No. 6.352, 15/07/1993).

Strategically distributed across various areas of the city to broaden access to the vulnerable population, there are currently four People's Restaurants and one canteen that promote equity over "fast culture." They provide cheap, healthy, safe and accessible food for all, made from fresh local produce. As reported by ICLEI in 2013, lunch costs 3 reals (about $1), half that price to the beneficiaries of the "Bolsa Família" (Family Basket) program, and free to the registered homeless – which represent about 160,000 people per year. In order to maintain the consistency of both price and quality, all the outlets are directly managed and administered by the municipality.

The program has allowed the community not only to make sure that the population is provided with fresh, nutritious food, but also to create a secure market for local farmers to sell their produce. According to Fondazione Giangiacomo Feltrinelli's report, Milan Urban Food Policy Pact, Belo's People's Restaurants serve almost 3 million meals annually.

VIEW THE FULL POLICY

• www.futurepolicy.org/food-and-water/belo-horizontes-food-security-policy

RESOURCES

• Article from ICLEI: www.iclei.org/details/article/belo-horizontes-popular-restaurants-end-urban-poverty.html

Improving Community Health Through Farmers Markets

New York, New York, U.S.

By Khushboo Balwani

Regular consumption of unhealthy foods and limited access to better options are two issues routinely affecting New York City's population. In order to address these, NYC has joined forces with the city's Department of Health, and together they have designed three key programs under their Farmers Markets strategy: Stellar Farmers Markets, Farmers Markets for Kids and Farm to Preschool.

The Stellar Farmers Markets program provides free, bilingual education workshops and cooking demonstrations and recipes at several farmers markets throughout the city, promoting the benefits of healthy eating and using locally grown, seasonal produce. As an incentive to attend the workshops, "Health Bucks" (coupons worth $2 each) are given to those participating in the National Supplemental Nutrition Assistance Program with Electronic Benefit Transfer (EBT) cards. These coupons can then be redeemed when buying fresh fruits and vegetables at all farmers markets across NYC.

In order to instill healthy eating habits in young consumers, NYC has two other initiatives: Farmers Markets for Kids and Farm to Preschool. The former focuses on bilingual, creative food workshops and hands-on activities, and the latter brings fresh, locally grown fruits and vegetables to participating New York City preschools, giving parents, staff and community members weekly access to fresh produce (which they can also pay for with Health Bucks and EBT cards). Farm to Preschool covers 11 locations across NYC, while Farmers Markets for Kids was hosted at two markets in South Bronx from July to October 2016. Stellar Farmers Markets is the largest municipal program providing access to fresh produce for low-income New Yorkers.

RESOURCES

- NYC Farmers Markets Strategy:
  www1.nyc.gov/site/doh/health/health-topics/cdp-farmersmarkets.page

- Stellar Farmer Markets program:
  www.grownyc.org/greenmarket/ebt/stellarmarkets

- Health Bucks program:
  www1.nyc.gov/site/doh/health/health-topics/health-bucks.page

Urban Family Gardens Growing Local Food Security

◊ Medellín, Colombia

—

By Khushboo Balwani

The goal of the "Huertas Familiares para Autoconsumo" (Urban Family Gardens) initiative is to provide vulnerable families with better access to healthy, fresh and nutritious food. The program enables these families, often displaced from rural areas, to achieve a certain level of self-sufficiency by granting them access to both the training and land necessary to grow their own vegetables for home consumption.

Conceived with a peer-learning structure in mind, the Urban Family Gardens take advantage of the knowledge and expertise of the participating families, building on their experiences to provide the training the group requires. A local-government appointed interdisciplinary panel including an agronomist, social workers and a nutritionist is also available to provide further support to the participants.

The program has been implemented in 13 of Medellín's 16 "comunas" (neighborhoods), reaching 150 vegetable gardens by 2013, which rose to 435 by 2014.

VIEW THE FULL POLICY

- (Spanish) www.medellin.gov.co/irj/go/km/docs/pccdesign/SubportaldelCiudadano_2/PlandeDesarrollo_0_15/InformacinGeneral/Shared%20Content/Documentos/instrumentos/ps/PLAN_SEGURIDAD_ALIMENTARIA_2016-2028.pdf

RESOURCES

- Extensive report by Fondazione Giangiacomo Feltrinelli: www.ruaf.org/sites/default/files/MUFPP_SelectedGoodPracticesfromCities.pdf

- Video explaining the program (Spanish): www.youtube.com/watch?v=0vAb2Qyssq8

- Global Compact Cities Program report: citiesprogramme.com/wp-content/uploads/2015/05/Case-Study-Medellin-Food-Security.pdf

4

WORK

New technologies, anti-labor trade liberalization, and economic instability have led to the volatile employment environment we have today. The shift to freelancing and portfolio-driven careers enabled by peer-to-peer platforms is offering extreme flexibility and an almost infinite choice to entrepreneurs who sell their services within a global marketplace. Notwithstanding that these digital service exchanges provide a lifeline to many underemployed workers, they provide little with regard to worker protection, health insurance, or even stable cash flow. People are working longer hours, for lower wages, and with less long-term income security.

Indeed, the combination of "zero hour" work contracts, transient employment, and increased global competition has significantly reduced workers' bargaining power. Add to this the fact that digital disruption is moving to reconfigure postindustrial economies as advances in robotics, machine learning, and automation promise a "Fourth Industrial Revolution" that could eliminate millions of jobs.

Mainstream economics argues that low wages and tax breaks for large corporations are the best way to attract investment and drive job growth. However, the cases and policies in this chapter tell another story. They demonstrate the ways in which entrepreneurs, communities, and cities are developing innovative solutions to generate local economic development and sustainable job creation through worker-owned cooperatives, startup collectives, open-value networks, and responsible sharing-based organizations.

Cities have an important role to play in setting the right incentives to encourage the growth of domestic sharing-based startups and raise public trust in using these services. For example, policies and investment support for worker-owned cooperatives can go a long way towards sustainable job creation.

Creative social entrepreneurs and digital-labor advocates are developing new ways of harnessing emerging technologies in order to allocate value on a more equitable basis. The emerging platform cooperatives movement, for example, is reclaiming worker solidarity, mutualism, and collective benefit as central tenets of a new commons economy.

Meanwhile, new technologies are driving marginal costs to zero, making it increasingly easy for many products and services to become available for free across distributed and collaborative networks. This democratization and decentralization of production and consumption is giving way to new work environments such as Fab Labs and collaborative work centers.

Building on these collaborative workspaces, social entrepreneurs have begun disrupting traditional business models and governance structures to create more distributive forms of value creation through shared budgeting and decision-making. Enspiral, for example, is a decentralized entrepreneurial collective that has spawned a stable of digital startups with a social impact mission.

Taken as a whole, the disruptive changes to work in the 21st century are complex and challenging. However, the examples profiled in this chapter demonstrate that workers, enterprises, and cities can work together, on their own terms, to increase prosperity, address inequality, and accelerate opportunities for value creation in the development of a more equitable future for all.

Darren Sharp and Khushboo Balwani

Enspiral:

A Network of Social Entrepreneurs Generating Shared Value for Mutual Benefit

⚲ Wellington, New Zealand (and worldwide)

By Darren Sharp

PROBLEM

It is often difficult for independent professionals interested in social-impact assignments to find meaningful projects. On-demand platforms, in which people often work remotely for little pay, can be isolating. How do freelancers who want to pursue community-oriented projects connect with other like-minded individuals?

SOLUTION

Enspiral, a decentralized entrepreneurial collective based in Wellington, New Zealand, began in 2010 with a goal of creating communities of workers who are deeply committed to social issues. Sometimes described as an "open-value network," Enspiral is a global coalition of enterprises that enables people to allocate their time and skills to social-impact projects by offering spaces and platforms that promote collaboration. The hub of the network is the Enspiral Foundation Limited, which holds common assets and facilitates interactions between members and related companies. Enspiral is an ongoing experiment in distributed leadership that includes more than 300 people and 22 different ventures in multiple countries. More than half the people involved in Enspiral are based in Wellington, with the rest dispersed across Australia, North America, Asia, and Europe.

> "Enspiral's greatest value is generated via the network's relational commons that is built on trust and social bonds, which creates a culture of solidarity and mutual support."

Alanna (Krause) Irving, co-founder of Loomio

While effective, Enspiral is not a simple cut-and-paste model that can easily be replicated. It is a shared set of tools and practices that demonstrates the potential for organically growing organizations from the bottom-up through an aligned sense of purpose. Enspiral includes a focus on activities that are hyperlocal in order to leverage situated strengths, a collaborative emphasis on sharing stories of best practices so that communities can learn together, and a platform for building open-source tools that can be used and adapted by others. Perhaps most importantly, Enspiral demonstrates the way in which values-aligned organizations can build and share resources in the context of social solidarity, and with a "reciprocity-first" ethos.

RESULTS

- The Enspiral network has spawned a number of open-source software projects and a knowledge commons of collaborative resources. Enspiral venture Loomio, for example, is a worker-owned cooperative that has developed an open-source app for consensus decision-making. Its 100,000 users include national governments, workplaces, and community organizations around the world. Loomio raised $450,000 in capped impact investment using "redeemable preference shares (RPS)" with no associated decision-making control, allowing the cooperative to maintain its autonomy, Yes! Magazine reported in 2016.

- Enspiral has also created its own internal economy to collaboratively allocate value, fund mission-aligned projects, and support the operational costs of its foundation. Internal contractors within Enspiral Services contribute 20 percent of the revenue they generate into a collective pool of funds. Enspiral Ventures also contributes to the foundation through negotiated "revenue-sharing agreements" which vary by company. Members then use an internal form of crowdfunding to distribute collective funds to worthy projects, which could be anything from hiring staff, paying for conference travel, or purchasing equipment.

RESOURCES

- Enspiral: www.enspiral.com
- Loomio: www.loomio.org
- Cobudget: cobudget.co

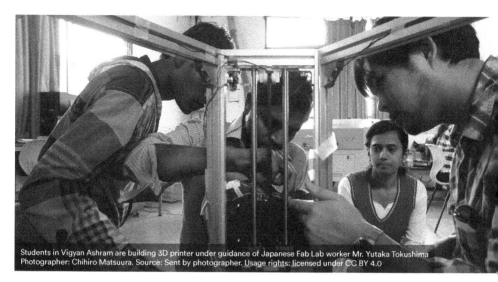

Students in Vigyan Ashram are building 3D printer under guidance of Japanese Fab Lab worker Mr. Yutaka Tokushima
Photographer: Chihiro Matsuura. Source: Sent by photographer. Usage rights: licensed under CC BY 4.0

Fab Labs:
Peer Production for a New Commons Economy

⚲ Pabal, India (and worldwide)

─────

By Khushboo Balwani

PROBLEM

How can consumers become producers? The shift from consumer culture to maker culture is often described in terms of a synthesis between consumers and producers – "prosumers." What practical steps can be taken for people to become prosumers?

SOLUTION

In 2002, Neil Gershenfeld, from the Massachusetts Institute of Technology (MIT), visited India to teach and explore projects that overlap with his work on fabrication labs or "Fab Labs." Responding to the challenges facing the local community, Gershenfeld suggested developing a Fab Lab in Vigyan Ashram, an education center for science located in Pabal, India. The organization has been working with the local community of Pabal since 1983 to solve problems in the region with the help of low-cost materials and traditional tools. With a focus on self-managed sustainability, it has enabled the development of new models of peer production and local entrepreneurship.

The first Fab Lab outside of MIT, the Vigyan Ashram Fab Lab worked with MIT in procuring the latest tools and machines for collaborative production, rather than

> "Thanks to the global network of Fab Labs, it is easy to tap into problems faster and to ask for support, such as technical help or knowledge sharing."

Dr. Yogesh Kulkarni, executive director of Vigyan Ashram

relying on ready-made solutions. Since then, several Fab Labs have been created worldwide. Indeed, today there are some 665 Fab Labs in 65 countries. Taken as a whole, Fab Lab is a distributed international network of scientific researchers and community inventors who define, conduct, and apply new discoveries and inventions for the benefit of both researchers and the local community. Fab Labs support a global design commons where members design, code, share knowledge, and create digital instruction manuals using open-source principles. What gets designed in one lab can theoretically be fabricated in another lab, anywhere in the world.

The projects at the Vigyan Ashram Fab Lab emerge either from local researchers or the local community. Once projects are conceived, the organization passes them to its students and opens a global discussion within the larger network of Fab Labs to leverage open designs and shared knowledge. Several prototypes are made locally and tested within the community using shared assets (space, knowledge, tools) until the final design is developed.

RESULTS

- The Vigyan Ashram Fab Lab has developed a number of innovative solutions to local problems, such as a pedal-powered generator, egg incubator, and weather data logger.

- Thanks to its proven solutions, the Vigyan Ashram Fab Lab has become a point of reference and a consultant to local and national authorities on urban challenges. Furthermore, it has inspired the government of India and the state government of Maharashtra to develop a plan to establish tinkering labs and innovation centers at both local and district levels, as reported by Yogesh Kulkarni, executive director of Vigyan Ashram.

RESOURCES

- Fab Lab Vigyan Ashram: vigyanashram.com/innerpages/FabLab.aspx

- The Fab Foundation: fabfoundation.org

Club Cultural Matienzo:
Creating a Vibrant Arts Scene in a Big City Through Collaboration

♀ Buenos Aires, Argentina

By Juan Manuel Aranovich and Agustín Jais *(Club Cultural Matienzo)*, **and Darren Sharp**

PROBLEM

Buenos Aires boasts a rich tradition of arts and culture. However, after the tragic deaths of 194 young people at the República Cromañón nightclub fire in 2004, non-commercial cultural projects became much less common. The city stopped issuing permits to small and medium-sized cultural spaces, and artists were faced with the challenge of having to pay to exhibit their artwork at existing commercial enterprises.

In response, new alternative spaces began to emerge with the goal of showcasing contemporary art, dance, music, plays, visual arts, literary events, and more. Without permits, however, centers were consistently closed down. Maintenance costs, as well as retail prices of supplies, remained high. Rather than going underground, alternative cultural venues sought to acquire public recognition in order to develop fair, legal, and professional conditions.

SOLUTION

Founded in November 2008, Club Cultural Matienzo (CCM) is a worker-managed, independent venue for the arts, culture, and community life in Buenos Aires. Together, a group of 80 members developed this financially successful enterprise through which they support events both on and off the club's premises.

"We did not know where we were heading or what we wanted to achieve, although we did know that we wanted collective work, an entity that would listen to the community."

Juan Manuel Aranovich

The 1,000-square-meter (3,280-square-feet) venue hosts a daily program of activities, including music, performing arts, literature, visual arts, cinema, design, and education. It is also the home of an online radio station and a bar.

Taking an active role in the development of local – and regional – activism and collaboration networks, Matienzo is both a platform for community action and a movement for social transformation, understanding the value of culture as an identity-building process. From the very beginning, the club's development has focused on identifying social challenges, organizing meetings in which to exchange ideas, and collaborating towards the generating solutions. With this in mind, the club has actively shared its formula for success, contributing to the growth of a number of local cultural ventures, as well as helped connect these to provide mutual support.

RESULTS

- The club has paved the way for the development of specialized legal nonprofits to work pro bono on cultural projects. This has led to better conditions for artistic development, a much more vibrant arts scene overall, and ultimately an agreement to guarantee fair conditions for all artists.

- There has been an 800 percent increase in the number of local cultural spaces. Attendance has grown similarly.

- Hundreds of new artists have entered the commercial circuit after having experienced an artistic growth in the alternative circuit.

- A new law was passed to enable the opening of cultural centers and independent theaters in the city.

- There has been a 30 percent drop in the cost of supplies as a result of pooling resources with other cultural spaces. New partnerships with commercial brands have been forged to support sector-specific spaces.

RESOURCES

- Club Cultural Matienzo (Spanish): www.ccmatienzo.com.ar

- Escena (Spanish): www.escena.com.ar

- MECA (Spanish): movimientomeca.com.ar

Evergreen:
Cooperative Ownership and Anchor Institutions to Build Community Wealth
⌖ Cleveland, Ohio, U.S.

—

By John Duda *(The Democracy Collaborative)*

Mainstream job-training programs are often too focused on employment opportunities that do not offer workers anything more than a wage. An alternative approach aligns public, nonprofit, and philanthropic resources to give workers real pathways to good jobs, and a stake in a democratized local economy. Evergreen is a network of worker cooperatives linked together by a nonprofit holding corporation with a mission to provide jobs, dignity, and cooperative ownership opportunities to historically marginalized communities. Worker cooperatives include a green industrial laundry, a solar installation and energy efficiency retrofitting company, and a large-scale commercial greenhouse. The linked-cooperative structure has enabled innovative approaches to workforce and neighborhood development including a home-buying program that has helped a substantial portion of Evergreen's worker-owners become homeowners.

Employing over 100 people and with annual revenues of over $6 million, Evergreen has contributed to demonstrating that inclusive cooperative-driven economic development is not a utopian fantasy or a marginal niche activity, but a viable and scalable approach to fighting inequality.

RESOURCES
• Evergreen Cooperatives: www.evgoh.com

Library at The Dock:
A Makerspace in a Public Library

♀ Melbourne, Australia

─────

By Darren Sharp

The types of jobs that will last through the mass automation of work in the coming century will be those where people can apply their creative and critical thinking skills to solve complex problems with the help of technology. To give people a chance at developing these skills, the city of Melbourne has created its first makerspace. Located inside Library at The Dock, a cultural community space built into the Victoria Harbor, it runs a range of free classes to help the community learn 3D printing, Arduino essentials, video editing, and introductory coding. The library also hosts Mini Make Days that profile local maker groups from across the city and provide the public with an opportunity to discover the latest trends in the maker movement. The makerspace is staffed by a team who encourage the entire community, including young children and students, to become better makers by learning new skills that can bring to life a range of digital, electronic, and fabrication projects.

RESOURCES

• Library at The Dock: www.melbourne.vic.gov.au/community/hubs-bookable-spaces/the-dock/library-at-the-dock/Pages/library-at-the-dock.aspx

Platform Cooperatives:
A Sharing Economy That Shares the Wealth

⚲ Worldwide

By Nathan Schneider *(University of Colorado Boulder)*

Among the major market disruptions introduced alongside "sharing economy" platforms like Uber and Airbnb is a systemic process of local disempowerment. The privatization of infrastructure – such as transportation and communication – has led to transfer of decision-making authority and wealth from local communities to corporate platforms and their investors. Nonetheless, the growing movement for "platform cooperativism," or the development of democratic ownership and governance of online platforms such as an app or website, offer cities an alternative to multinational corporations that supports community wealth building. Examples of successful platform co-ops include Modo, a Vancouver, Canada-based carsharing cooperative, Stocksy United, an artist-owned cooperative that sells stock-photography online, and Green Taxi Cooperative in Denver, Colorado.

RESOURCES

- Platform Cooperativism Consortium: platform.coop

- The Internet of Ownership: ioo.coop

"

SHARE YOUR KNOWLEDGE. IT IS A WAY TO ACHIEVE IMMORTALITY.

– THE DALAI LAMA

Seoul Metropolitan Government Ordinance on the Promotion of Sharing

◉ Seoul, South Korea

––

By Darren Sharp

In 2012, Seoul Metropolitan Government (SMG) launched the Sharing City Seoul program and enacted the Seoul Metropolitan Government Ordinance on the Promotion of Sharing as the legal foundation for this world-leading initiative. The purpose of the ordinance is to "maximize utilization of resources, recover communities and revitalize the regional economy" by promoting sharing. The ordinance defines sharing as "activities that create social, economic and environmental values by jointly using resources, such as space, goods, information, talent and experience."

The ordinance designates official sharing enterprises that address urban challenges and meet social, economic, or environmental criteria. It is the legal basis for SMG's support – through funding, promotion, and capacity building – of qualifying, local sharing startups and nonprofit organizations.

More specifically, the mayor of Seoul may designate an organization that intends to solve social problems through sharing as a "sharing organization" or "sharing enterprise" following deliberations by the Sharing Promotion Committee of the SMG. The mayor may also provide funds from SMG's Small and Medium Enterprises Fund, and allow a sharing organization or enterprise to use a public facility at a reduced fee where necessary to serve the public interest.

VIEW THE FULL POLICY

- legal.seoul.go.kr/legal/english/front/page/law.html?pAct=lawView&pPromNo=1191

RESOURCES

- SMG's description of Sharing City Seoul:
  english.seoul.go.kr/policy-information/key-policies/city-initiatives/1-sharing-city

- Sharehub's in-depth 2016 report on Sharing City Seoul: english.sharehub.kr/e-book

Worker Cooperative Business Development Initiative

◉ New York, New York, U.S.

—

By Darren Sharp

The financial crisis of 2007-08 saw the substantial loss of full-time and living-wage jobs in many cities, including New York, with most newly created jobs being low-wage and part-time. In fiscal year 2015, the New York City Department of Small Business Services (SBS) launched the Worker Cooperative Business Development Initiative (WCBDI) as a way to reduce poverty and income inequality through support of worker-owned cooperatives.

The city council included funding in its $75 billion fiscal year 2015 budget to support the expansion of worker cooperatives throughout the city to help low-income New Yorkers become business owners. The council allocated $1.2 million in municipal investment through WCBDI across 10 partner organizations to support existing worker cooperatives, kick-start the creation of new worker cooperatives, and assist small businesses conversion to worker-owned models.

WCBDI has led to the creation of 21 new worker cooperatives, doubling their number in New York City, and has built the capacity of existing cooperatives through education, training, technical assistance, and funds. It is estimated that over 141 new worker-owner jobs have been created and over 900 entrepreneurs have received training in co-op development. This initial success encouraged the New York City Council to increase the initiative's funding to $2.1 million for fiscal year 2016.

VIEW THE FULL POLICY

- council.nyc.gov/budget/wp-content/uploads/sites/54/2014/07/fy2015-FY15-Schedule-C-Template-Final.pdf

RESOURCES

- WCBDI's 2015 report on their first year of operation, including the major impacts: www.nyc.gov/html/sbs/downloads/misc/wcbdi2015-booklet/offline/wcbdi.pdf

- Related change in New York's administrative code to support the effort: legistar.council.nyc.gov/LegislationDetail.aspx?ID=1853950&GUID=917F9D68-6081-4BE0-BABA-B9910461817F

- Report that influenced advocacy for worker cooperatives in New York City: institute.coop/sites/default/files/resources/432-Worker-Cooperatives-for-New-York-City-A-Vision-for-Addressing-Income-Inequality-FPWF-January2013.pdf

Procomuns: City Policies for the Commons Collaborative Economy

♀ Barcelona, Spain

———

By Mayo Fuster Morell, director of Dimmons.net, a digital commons research group at the Internet Interdisciplinary Institute (IN3), part of the Open University of Catalonia (UOC), and faculty affiliated at the Berkman Klein Center for Internet and Society, at Harvard University

The commons collaborative economy refers to collaborative consumption, production, sharing, and exchange among distributed groups of peers – supported by a digital platform – in conditions that empower them and society as a whole. The concept is in direct contrast to extractionist and explorative modalities, represented by companies like Uber and Airbnb. The commons collaborative economy results from the encounter of four trajectories of socio-economic innovation and democratization: the social and solidarity economy, including the cooperative tradition; the open knowledge of the commons; the environmental sustainability of the circular economy; and the gender perspectives of the feminist economy. Its enterprises support fair, sustainable, inclusive, and distributed patterns. Its business, governance models, and philosophy place the citizens in the central role as producers and decision makers in the economy, and ensure that economic growth is connected to the needs of society.

Barcelona city government believes that the commons collaborative economy is better for city residents than the commercial-oriented collaborative economy; hence it is promoting it as such. Moreover, the city council considers collaborative economy policies should be produced collaboratively. It was for this purpose that it formed BarCola, a working group between Barcelona City Council and the city's commons collaborative economy sector, represented by 20 enterprises. It was also why it supported the organization of Procomuns, a forum for policy co-creation.

Procomuns has developed and proposed over 120 related policy recommendations for Barcelona, including specific measures related to work. These recommendations are informed by the research of the Dimmons group at IN3 (Open University of Catalonia), the P2PValue Project, and the Procomuns conference co-organized by Barcelona City Council in March 2016. The goal of these policy recommendations is to promote fair, respectful and nonexploitative working conditions, particularly in collaborative economy projects. This includes the elimination of labor exploitation, sexual harassment, and gender gaps. This also includes the protection of "responsible citizen producers" as a new agent that generates the economic and social commons, and the fighting of corruption and "revolving doors" in the collaborative economy policy field.

These policy recommendations have been embraced by Barcelona's city council. An implementation plan for the citizen-approved policies has been drawn up and funded, and the implementation phase has begun. Furthermore, the policies are not the only thing of interest: the highly collaborative policy formulation process is also worth noting.

VIEW THE FULL POLICY

- procomuns.net/en/policy

RESOURCES

- Summary of the policy including the 10 policies that received more citizen support: procomuns.net/wp-content/uploads/2016/03/ CommonsDeclarationPolicies_eng_v03_summary.pdf

- Procomuns videos: procomuns.net/en/streaming-videos

- Interview detailing the collaborative policy development process: www.shareable.net/blog/barcelona-crowdsourced-its-sharing-economy-policies-can-other-cities-do-the-same

Public Services (Social Value) Act 2012

♀ Multiple Locations, U.K.

——

By Khushboo Balwani

Social policy legislation enables new methods and practices for inclusion and community development. The Public Services (Social Value) Act of 2012 requires local authority commissioners to account for the social, environmental and economic well-being of an area when designing a service (i.e., pre-procurement), or when deciding to award a bid. This has enabled social enterprises and charities with a social mission to grow and contribute to job creation. According to a study by Social Enterprise UK, some local governments have gone a step further, developing new ways of commissioning, such as reduced management fees and advanced payment, as a means of encouraging social enterprises who lack significant capital to participate.

One example, as published by The Guardian, is Wakefield Council. When seeking a milk supplier for the local schools, the procurement officers selected Fresh Pastures, a social enterprise emphasizing healthy living, good dietary planning, recycling and job opportunities for the long-term unemployed. Similar social-value practices that overlap organizations supporting training and job opportunities for underprivileged groups are also being explored.

VIEW THE FULL POLICY

• www.legislation.gov.uk/ukpga/2012/3/enacted

RESOURCES

• Official policy note: www.legislation.gov.uk/ukpga/2012/3/enacted

Creative Spaces Cultural Policy

⚲ Sydney, Australia

—

By Darren Sharp

The city of Sydney's "Creative City Cultural Policy and Action Plan 2014 – 2024" contains a comprehensive set of policies to give artists and creative startups access to empty space through its Creative Spaces program. This culture-led revitalization initiative includes a strategic priority to create – as the policy outlines – "Precinct Distinctiveness and Creativity in the Public Domain" through actions that "broker space-based projects with the business community to encourage the use of empty office, retail and other commercial space by creative practitioners." In order to help activate creative neighborhoods, the city of Sydney also runs a program that provides affordable studio and workspace options, offering a range of properties owned by the city through short, medium and long-term leases.

VIEW THE FULL POLICY

- www.cityofsydney.nsw.gov.au/__data/assets/pdf_file/0011/213986/11418-Finalisation-of-Cultural-Policy-Document-July-2016.pdf

One-Stop-Shop for Social Clauses ('Guichet Unique des Clauses Sociales')

◊ Rennes Metropole, France

―

By Darren Sharp

Rennes Metropole, the capital city of Brittany (France), has instituted a public procurement policy to help people with low skill levels who are experiencing long-term unemployment. Using social clauses, the "guichet unique des clauses sociales" scheme requires companies who bid on city contracts to create social inclusion initiatives for any services provided to the city. For example, the social enterprise La Feuille d'Erable runs "back to work" programs for the long-term unemployed through the waste management and recycling services it provides to Rennes Metropole. They hire individuals for six to 24 months and provide them with additional career advice, training, and support to assist with future job prospects. In 2014, the social clauses in Rennes Metropole's public procurement policy helped 550 people work 260,000 hours, the equivalent of 157 full-time jobs.

VIEW THE FULL POLICY
● (French)
www.meif-bassinrennes.fr/territoire/clauses-sociales-grands-chantiers.html

RESOURCES
● Eurocities report: nws.eurocities.eu/MediaShell/media/green_jobs_for_social_inclusion_intro_FINAL.pdf

"

THERE IS NO DELIGHT IN OWNING ANYTHING UNSHARED.

– SENECA

5

ENERGY

The energy infrastructure that we inherited from the
20th century is one dominated by fossil fuels and
uranium, mined in relatively few localities in the world.
The distribution and refining of these fuels is tightly
held by a few large corporations. Electricity generation
typically occurs in plants that hold local or regional
monopolies, with vast profit potential. While gasoline is
burned in millions of vehicles, the distribution system
remains within the control of a few corporations, which
often have regional or national oligopoly or monopoly
control. The environmental impacts of the energy
industry are staggering. It is high time for change.

On the positive side, the need for change to a 21st century energy system based on renewable sources of energy is widely recognized, the necessary technologies exist (and are often cheaper than conventional forms of energy provision), and considerable progress has been made. We can build locally-based renewable energy infrastructures. Renewable energy from the sun, wind, water, organic waste, and geothermal heat can be found everywhere on the planet. Hence, every city and town can make use of available renewable energy sources that offer economic opportunity and enhance resilience in the face of global economic crises and environmental change. On a regional level, localities can exchange energy in order to even out seasonal or daily imbalances in supply and demand.

A locally based vision of renewable energy generation could eliminate global- or national-level domination of the energy infrastructure by a few large players, and thus the concentration of profits in the hands of a very few. It could also reduce our greenhouse gas emissions to very low levels, comparable to the emissions before the industrial revolution. But the local orientation alone would not ensure that the benefits would be shared among all sectors of the local population, and therefore it would not guarantee widespread and active support. This is where sharing solutions come in. Shared energy infrastructure means that people together own and operate both the distributed energy generation facilities and the infrastructure to deliver that energy from where it is generated to where it is used.

In a sharing vision of a local renewable energy system, many households will generate their own renewable energy (as in solar photovoltaic or solar thermal systems on their rooftops), but many more, for whom this is not an option, will share in the ownership and operation of off-site renewable energy generation infrastructure such as wind turbines. The distribution systems by which energy is delivered to households will belong to cooperatives, municipalities, or trusts that are accountable to their customers and therefore do not take advantage of the potential of supply monopolies to generate economic rents (unearned income; extraordinary profits). The energy infrastructure is built by companies controlled by their employees, ensuring equitable sharing of the economic benefits. The construction and maintenance of this entire infrastructure is financed in such a way that it benefits the producers and consumers (and often prosumers – people who both produce and consume what they produce), rather than simply providing growth opportunities for the finance "industry." Consumers use their buying power to ensure that they obtain renewable energy that is produced under fair conditions.

All the elements of this locally-based, sharing vision of a renewable energy infrastructure already exist. Some have even been brought to considerable scale, as for example in Denmark, where a large proportion of the wind energy generation is accomplished by local wind cooperatives. The challenge is to bring all these elements together into mutually supportive networks, and to establish such networks essentially everywhere.

In this chapter, we portray examples of some of the key elements, focusing on those that can be implemented at the urban scale – while recognizing that it is also essential to work at the national and international levels. Shared ownership is fundamental throughout. In many countries, much of the grid is owned by municipal authorities, which is an excellent solution as long as democratic accountability of these authorities is ensured. Unfortunately, there has been a trend in recent years to privatize electric distribution grids, on the basis of the argument that private control is automatically more "efficient." However, this argument is only valid if there is true market competition, which is not the case in most energy distribution systems.

In this context, the best way to ensure that a business serves its customers is for the customers to take over the business. There are different models to do this: in rural areas – as in much of the U.S. – rural electric cooperatives have long played a large role in running the local grids. In large urban areas, however, this model has not been as successful. At the urban scale, municipal ownership or trusts are more prevalent.

Finally, it is important that the workers installing all this equipment get a good deal – and this works best if they themselves own their own companies and make the important decisions. The challenge now is to bring all these elements together and help them to grow, in order to build an energy infrastructure that allows all of us to live well, while ensuring good living conditions for all the other species on this planet.

Wolfgang Hoeschele

Citizens submitting signatures at the City Hall of Hamburg, petitioning for the referendum for the municipal government to re-acquire its privatized energy infrastructure, 2011. Source: Bund für Umwelt und Naturschutz Deutschland (BUND). Usage rights: CC BY 1.0

Residents of Hamburg Reclaim the Power Grid

◊ Hamburg, Germany

By Wolfgang Hoeschele

PROBLEM

From 2000 to 2014, the energy infrastructure of the city of Hamburg was mainly in the hands of private energy monopolies – such as Vattenfall and E.On – that controlled most of Germany's electric power infrastructure. These companies had a strong interest in utilizing their coal and nuclear power plants as long as possible, thereby obstructing a shift to renewable energies. Moreover, they were reluctant to provide equal access to small power providers and invest in a smart grid that allows more effective management of variable, distributed power inputs. Owing to these factors, progress to lower Hamburg's greenhouse gas emissions was being stalled. What could citizens do?

SOLUTION

A citizen's movement emerged in Hamburg for the city to buy back the energy infrastructure. In spite of strong opposition from the ruling party, the movement successfully organized for a referendum to be held on the matter, which passed in 2013. As a result, Hamburg bought back the electric distribution network from Vattenfall in early 2014, signed a contract to buy back the gas distribution network from E.On by 2018, and is negotiating the purchase of the district heating network by 2019.

The electric distribution system (Stromnetz Hamburg) is now owned 100 percent by the city of Hamburg, which means that its activities are overseen by representatives of the city government. A consumer's advisory council has been formed, which has been holding several meetings annually since 2014. In order to establish more democratic control of the entire energy distribution network, a multi-stakeholder advisory council – comprised of representatives of all major political parties as well as the organizations that campaigned for the recommunalization of the energy infrastructure – has been established.

RESULTS

- According to Manfred Braasch, managing director of BUND (Friends of the Earth Germany) and leader of the campaign to buy back the energy infrastructure, while it's still too early to fully assess the impacts of this change of ownership, the new management has made a strong commitment to expanding renewable energy sources and, in contrast to Vattenfall, is proactively investing in a sustainable and smart grid.

- Though the advisory council lacks executive power, it should be noted that Stromnetz Hamburg is accountable to the elected city government. Thus, it is up to the voters to elect responsible political leaders.

- An online energy portal allows the public to track how much solar and wind power is being produced in Hamburg on a daily basis, and to compare predicted production with actual production. Progress toward goals for renewable energy generation can also be monitored on this website, building in additional layers of public engagement and accountability.

RESOURCES

- Contracts and other information concerning implementation of the referendum (German): www.hamburg.de/energiewende/downloads

- Energy Portal of Stromnetz Hamburg GmbH (German): www.energieportal-hamburg.de/distribution/energieportal

- Bylaws of the Energy Advisory Council (German): www.buergerschaft-hh. de/ParlDok/dokument/51900/stellungnahme-des-senats-zu-den-ersuchen-der-b%C3%BCrgerschaft-vom-28-mai-2015-einrichtung-eines-politischen-stromnetzbeirates-drucksache-21-493-.pdf

Danish Wind Turbines. Photographer: www.CGPGrey.com, Source: www.CGPGrey.com. Usage rights: Creative Commons Attribution 2.0 Generic

Wind Energy Cooperative Enables Citizens to Produce Their Own Clean Energy

♀ Copenhagen, Denmark

By Wolfgang Hoeschele

PROBLEM

The establishment of a carbon-neutral energy system requires massive investments in infrastructure, such as wind turbines. Because distributed energy systems do not fit the business models of the old energy utilities, they continue to invest far too little in this sector. Meanwhile, many individual electric power consumers are interested in investing in renewable power infrastructure, but these investments are too large and require a level of expertise too advanced for individual households to be able to support them. How can consumers take matters into their own hands?

SOLUTION

Wind cooperatives allow multiple households to pool their funds to collectively build one or more wind turbines. As co-owners, they make investment decisions and negotiate the terms with operators of larger electric networks.

An urban example of this is the Middelgrunden Wind Turbine Cooperative, formed in 1997, which partnered with the Copenhagen municipal utility to build 20 wind turbines of 2MW capacity each, off the shore of Copenhagen. Københavns Energi, the municipal partner, has since then merged with several other companies to form the private energy company DONG Energy. The cooperative owns 10 of the turbines, while the other 10 are owned by DONG Energy. Over 8,500 people who mostly live in or around Copenhagen own the 40,500 shares of the co-op. The cooperative is organized as a partnership, and each partner has one vote, regardless of the number of shares. One wind turbine is a "children's wind turbine" – shareholders have had their children vote on their behalf and thereby participate in the decision-making process, learning how to organize a sustainable future as cooperation between people.

The cooperative benefits from the support of the Danish association of owners of wind turbines (founded in 1978 as Danske Vindkraftvaerker, later renamed Danmarks Vindmølleforening). This association has successfully lobbied the national government to create favorable conditions for the expansion of wind energy. In part due to its activities, cooperatives accounted for around 50 percent of Danish installed wind energy capacity in the 1980s to early 1990s, and 20 percent of installed capacity today.

RESULTS

- The wind turbines were completed by 2001, and the output of the cooperative's turbines has been varying from 40-45,000 MWh in the last several years.

- This is one of many examples in Denmark of wind power being produced as a result of the collective efforts of individuals interested in wind power.

- There is high public support for wind power in Denmark, due in no small part to the fact that ordinary people, not just some distant shareholders, are direct beneficiaries.

RESOURCES

- FEASTA report on Denmark's wind cooperatives: feasta.org/documents/shortcircuit/index.html?sc5/windguilds.html

- Middelgrunden cooperative bylaws: www.middelgrunden.dk/middelgrunden/?q=en/node/72

- English translation of Danish Promotion of Renewable Energy Act of 2008: ens.dk/sites/ens.dk/files/Vindenergi/promotion_of_renewable_energy_act_-_extract.pdf

Community Purchasing Alliance Reduces Energy and Other Bills for Member Organizations

♀ Washington, D.C., U.S.

By Wolfgang Hoeschele

PROBLEM

Religious, social, and educational institutions often spend excessive amounts of money on energy and other services, straining their limited budgets. At the same time, they often buy these services from companies with no better than average environmental and social responsibility, contradicting the central mission of these institutions.

SOLUTION

Founded in 2011, the Community Purchasing Alliance (CPA) uses the combined purchasing power of a large number of social, religious, and educational institutions in the Washington, D.C., area in order to be able to negotiate for better terms, saving each institution some thousands of dollars every year. In their negotiations, CPA also draws on the expertise of the membership of participating institutions.

In addition to obtaining better financial deals, the CPA has established four sets of criteria for the companies with which they do business: environmental, worker justice (wages, health benefits, treatment of workers, union labor or not, where and who they hire from, part-time/full-time), community-wealth building (priority to businesses owned by women and people of color, as well as cooperatives), and

> "Faith based organizations have tremendous financial resources and they have used their investments for decades to foster social change. Through the Community Purchasing Alliance cooperative I have learned that they can achieve similar economic and social impact by combining their purchasing power."

Paul Hazen, president of the board of the directors of the Community Purchasing Alliance

other local community or social impact. The organization is also exploring possibilities to invest in energy efficiency. Thus, the purchasing power of the participating institutions supports a more sustainable local economy.

For example, the group arranges for the purchase of electric power from renewable sources with Green-e certified renewable energy credits (RECs) and for the installation of solar photovoltaic panels on rooftops without upfront costs (the installation costs are paid out of the later savings). For installing solar, they ask about workers, wages, education, job training and other, but because the solar developers and installers in the Washington, D.C., area all perform well on these criteria, to date the evaluation has been primarily based on price and quality considerations.

The organization itself is a cooperative owned by its member institutions, meaning that it is directly accountable to the institutions it serves. Sixty percent of its net margins are devoted to community organizing and other community-based, cooperative-development initiatives.

RESULTS
- According to the CPA website, there are now 145 participating organizations, which have collectively saved $584,000 in 2015.
- Fourty-four million kWh have been switched to renewable energy.

RESOURCES
- Community Purchasing Alliance: cpa.coop
- Shareable article: https://www.shareable.net/blog/how-a-startup-dc-purchasing-co-op-saved-members-1-million

SolarShare Bond:

Renewable Energy Investment Cooperative for Local Commercial Scale Projects

⦿ Ontario, Canada

—

By Emily Skeehan

Governments around the world still subsidize polluting, carbon-based energy projects, totaling hundreds of billions of dollars per year, according to The New York Times. In addition to this, the Financial Times has reported how these incentives are not yet offered to renewable energy systems at nearly the same scale. In response, entrepreneurs are creating alternative models to build distributed grids that derive power from clean energy sources and financial support directly from their local community members.

In Canada, residents of Ontario can invest in local solar power projects by buying SolarShare bonds. SolarShare is a renewable energy cooperative that enables anyone living in Ontario to invest in solar power projects in the area and become a voting member of the co-op. The minimum buy-in for SolarShare bonds is $1,000 Canadian dollars (around $740) for a 5-year term at 5 percent fixed interest, and CA$10,000 (just over $7,400) for a 15-year term at 6 percent fixed interest. Investors who purchase 5-year bonds receive an annual return through semiannual interest payments until the term of their investment ends, at which point they receive their entire principal investment. The 15-year bonds are self-amortizing, so each semi-annual payment is made up of both principal and interest. The investor-members collectively vote in their board members, and can serve on one of the co-op's many committees. SolarShare has completed 39 solar installation projects and is on track to build eight more through 2017. The cooperative will own solar assets worth more than CA$55 million (over $40 million) by fall 2017.

RESOURCES

- SolarShare: www.solarbonds.ca

- New York Times article: www.nytimes.com/2015/12/06/science/on-tether-to-fossil-fuels-nations-speak-with-money.html

- Financial Times article:
  www.ft.com/content/fb264f96-5088-11e6-8172-e39ecd3b86fc

Namasté Solar:
Solar Worker Cooperative Shares Economic Benefits of the Renewable Energy Transition with Workers

◊ Multiple Locations, U.S.

By Wolfgang Hoeschele

The construction of sustainable infrastructure for renewable-energy projects is a source of immense economic opportunity. The workers who install these new systems, however, tend to gain relatively little from the creation of this wealth. Worker cooperatives are one way to ensure that the benefits of the renewable energy transition are shared more equally. Namasté Solar, based out of Colorado, began as an employee-owned benefit company when it was founded in 2005, but formally shifted to a cooperative structure in 2011. To become a worker-owner of the cooperative, candidates work with Namasté Solar for a year to determine whether they are the right match. If they are, employees buy a share in the cooperative and earn voting rights in their decision-making process. When business is going well, extra earnings are divided among the worker-owners. Namasté Solar has over 100 worker-owners across four offices in Colorado, California, and New York. The co-op has begun undertaking many big solar installations in Colorado, including a convention center, a hospital, and a museum.

RESOURCES
• Namasté Solar: www.namastesolar.com

Auckland Energy Consumer Trust:
Exercising Public Oversight and Profit Sharing Among Electricity Consumers

◉ Auckland, New Zealand

By Wolfgang Hoeschele

Public utilities require proper public oversight to ensure that the entities operating them do not exploit their monopoly positions to drive up costs for the communities they serve. In addition to regulatory oversight, another way to instigate public accountability is the creation of trusts, which put control over the utility in the hands of the people. In 1993, New Zealand established the Auckland Energy Consumer Trust (AECT) to own and oversee the companies that operate the electricity distribution networks. AECT was one of 30 energy trusts that the New Zealand government established following national reforms to its electricity system.

In 2016, it was renamed to Entrust. Entrust owns a majority share of Vector, the largest electricity distribution company in New Zealand. Entrust equally distributes profit dividends from Vector to all of its beneficiaries, over 320,000 households and businesses across the country. The beneficiaries, who are all customers of Vector, vote trustees into office. Two of Entrust's trustees serve on Vector's board of directors to monitor the company's performance. This system ensures that the monopoly energy provider serves the consumer's interests. If excessive bills were charged, the profits would ultimately be returned to the consumers.

RESOURCES
• Entrust: www.entrustnz.co.nz

"

THE MIRACLE IS THIS: THE MORE WE SHARE, THE MORE WE HAVE.

— *LEONARD NIMOY*

Barcelona Fights Climate Change with Building Ordinance Requiring Solar Thermal Technology to Heat Water

♀ Barcelona, Spain

By Ana Marques *(ICLEI)*, Toni Pujol *(Barcelona City Council)* and Emily Skeehan

Adapted from this ICLEI case: www.iclei.org/fileadmin/PUBLICATIONS/Case_Studies/ICLEI_cs_173_Barcelona_UrbanLEDS_2014.pdf

In 2000, Barcelona became the first European city to implement a Solar Thermal Ordinance (STO), making it compulsory to use solar energy to supply 60 percent of running hot water in all new buildings, renovated buildings, and buildings changing their use, independently of whether they are privately or publicly owned. The STO is part of Barcelona's long-term strategy, integrated in a political and planning framework for climate change mitigation, to achieve energy self-sufficiency in the long term through the promotion of energy efficiency and the use of renewable resources. In addition, Barcelona offers a housing tax incentive for voluntary solar (thermal or photovoltaic) installations, regulated by the Municipal Fiscal Ordinance. The incentive provides a 50 percent tax reduction for four years after installation.

The STO applies to buildings that are intended for residential purposes, health, sports, commercial, industrial, and any other use that entails the presence of dining rooms, kitchens or collective laundries. With the approval of the Barcelona Environmental Ordinance in 2011, the scope was extended to require the use of solar energy (photovoltaics) for electricity generation in the design of new and renovated buildings.

The approval of the STO has created new market opportunities. Requests for the installation of solar thermal systems has increased, and so has the total surface area of solar thermal systems in the city from 1,650 square meters (over 1 square mile) in 2000 to 87,600 square meters (54.4 square miles) in 2010, increasing the licensed surface by a factor of more than 50 times. This has created projected energy savings of over 11,200 MWh per year, and resulted in a reduction of greenhouse gas emissions of approximately 1,970 tonnes (2,171 US tons) of CO_2 per year, further contributing to Barcelona's energy independence. More than 50 other Spanish cities have replicated the ordinance.

VIEW THE FULL POLICY

- 2014 modifications to Barcelona's 2011 Environmental Ordinance (Catalan): w110.bcn.cat/Ajuntament/Continguts/Ordenances/medi_ambient_mod1.pdf

RESOURCES

- Barcelona's energy, climate change, and air quality plan for 2011-2020: w110.bcn.cat/MediAmbient/Continguts/Vectors_Ambientals/Energia_i_ qualitat_ambiental/Documents/Traduccions/PECQ_english_def01.pdf

Scotland Promotes Local, Shared Ownership of Renewable Energy Infrastructure

♀ Multiple Locations, Scotland

By Wolfgang Hoeschele

In 2011, the Scottish government established the policy goal to dramatically reduce its reliance on nonrenewable energy sources. According to its 2020 Routemap for Sustainable Energy in Scotland, "community benefits and scope for local ownership of energy are key elements of public engagement in renewables, helping to change cultural attitudes to renewables as well as to generate local revenue as part of the green low carbon economy."

Accordingly, the Scottish government established a target of 500 MW community and locally owned renewable energy capacity by 2020. This is small compared to the total 15,000 MW target, but large compared to the 180 MW of existing, planned, or under construction local projects in 2011.

To help reach the target, Local Energy Scotland, a consortium of several different institutions, established a web portal with a comprehensive set of tools and resources for communities and rural businesses that want to start renewable energy projects. It includes an interactive map of existing projects, access to free advice, a comprehensive guide to shared ownership of projects, and more.

In 2015, the 500 MW target of local renewable energy capacity was achieved. This target may not have been ambitious, but the support base is there to greatly exceed it.

VIEW THE FULL POLICY
- 2020 Routemap for Sustainable Energy in Scotland:
  www.gov.scot/Publications/2011/08/04110353/0

RESOURCES
- Local Energy Scotland: www.localenergyscotland.org

- Guide to shared ownership of local, renewable energy projects:
  www.localenergyscotland.org/good-practice/shared-ownership

Nelson Mandela Bay Municipality Leads South Africa in Small-scale Embedded Energy Generation

⚲ Nelson Mandela Bay Municipality, South Africa

By **Elana Keef** *(Afri-Coast Engineers SA)* and **Emily Skeehan**

Adapted from this ICLEI case: www.iclei.org/fileadmin/PUBLICATIONS/Case_Studies/ICLEI_cs_174_NMBM_UrbanLEDS_2014.pdf

South Africa's electricity demand exceeds supply. Rolling blackouts are frequently necessary and there are growing concerns about climate change. In 2011, the National Energy Regulator of South Africa (NERSA) developed and approved the Standard Conditions for Small-scale Embedded Generation (SSEG) within Municipal Boundaries. Embedded generation refers to the generation of electricity from renewable sources by residents, business, or industries via grid-connected devices. Now, local providers with generation systems smaller than 100 kW no longer require a generation license, and the specifications and standards for connecting to the grid have been simplified.

In addition, Nelson Mandela Bay Municipality (NMBM) is facilitating embedded generation through an accessible application process and minimal cost requirements (net-metering and covering 50 percent of the cost of bi-directional meters). Moreover, a tax incentive for businesses allows organizations to depreciate renewable energy assets within three years. To date, 27 embedded generation systems have been connected to the NMBM grid, with 25 of these systems being smaller than 100 kW. The local community is actively involved in energy generation; a significant portion of Nelson Mandela Bay's electricity is now generated by local renewable energy generation systems.

This policy lays a foundation for low-carbon urban growth, economic and socio-economic development, improved energy security through the diversification of the local energy mix, better services for the community, and a safer and healthier environment for residents. Yet, a clear national framework for SSEG would facilitate implementation by other municipalities. More local control over energy supply and planning would give independent power producers fair access to both the national and local grid.

RESOURCES

- www.iclei.org/fileadmin/PUBLICATIONS/Case_Studies/ICLEI_cs_174_NMBM_UrbanLEDS_2014.pdf

Community Solar Gardens

◊ State of Minnesota, U.S.

By Wolfgang Hoeschele

In 2013, the state of Minnesota developed a program to promote "community solar gardens" in which utility customers purchase shares of local solar photovoltaic energy facilities. This was designed to address a problem many people in the state were facing: they would like to use renewable energy, but cannot install their own solar systems either because they rent the property where they live, or because they do not own a house or building on which a solar array can be effectively installed. The state has made the process as simple and transparent as possible. As a result of this policy, a large number of solar cooperatives have been formed. According to Xcel Energy's October 2016 monthly update on community solar gardens to the Minnesota Public Utilities Commission, applications have been filed for 214 project sites since 2013, including 85 projects being designed and 33 projects in the construction phase of the Solar*Rewards Community process.

VIEW THE FULL POLICY

• Summary of Minnesota's renewable energy legislation of 2013:
  www.house.leg.state.mn.us/hrd/pubs/ss/sssolarleg.pdf

RESOURCES

• Specific provisions regarding solar gardens:
  www.revisor.mn.gov/statutes/?id=216B.1641

• Local government toolkit for community solar:
  www.cleanenergyresourceteams.org/solargardens/toolkit

• Minneapolis renewable energy plans: www.ci.minneapolis.mn.us/www/groups/
  public/@citycoordinator/documents/webcontent/wcms1p-121587.pdf

Feed-in-Tariffs

⌖ Multiple Locations, Germany

—

By Wolfgang Hoeschele

Feed-in-Tariffs (FITs) are guaranteed prices for electric energy from renewable sources sold by small producers into the grid. Without FITs, small producers often are at the mercy of distribution networks that are not interested in buying electric power from them, greatly reducing the economic viability of small-scale investments in renewable energy by individuals or cooperatives. A FIT-policy was enacted in Germany, which led to the rapid expansion of distributed renewable electric generation. According to Future Policy, "the production of electricity from renewable sources in Germany was only 6.2 percent in 2000, increasing to 23.7 percent by 2012 and up to about 28 percent in 2014."

In fact, while FITs can result in excessive spending for too little generating capacity if they are not adapted to declining production costs, they do allow a (controversial) process of establishing at a community or national level what is regarded as a fair price, considering not only the market, but also environmental and social factors. It is thus important that a multiplicity of relevant stakeholders be involved in setting the actual levels of the FITs and adjusting them to changing conditions.

VIEW THE FULL POLICY
• www.clearingstelle-eeg.de/files/node/8/EEG_2012_Englische_Version.pdf

RESOURCES
• Analysis of Germany's FIT regulation: www.futurepolicy.org/climate-stability/ renewable-energies/the-german-feed-in-tariff

Community Choice Aggregation

◊ Multiple Locations, U.S.

—

By John Farrell *(Institute for Local Self-Reliance)* **and Emily Skeehan**

While cities increasingly have the desire to move away from the use of fossil fuels, many are facing obstacles in converting their electricity supplies to clean energy. According to CDP, which surveys the world's cities regarding climate change, just 35 percent of all cities report that they have set a renewable energy target.

A policy called "community choice aggregation" allows local governments (or groups of local governments) to join together to make energy-purchasing decisions on behalf of residential and small business customers in their community. In practice, it means that cities can choose their energy suppliers on the basis of cost, pollution, and local economic benefits, without having to own and maintain the electric grid.

The Community Choice Aggregation (CCA) process helps cities to aggregate demand for nonfossil electricity and use it to negotiate contracts with electricity suppliers. Cities are participating in CCA with the goal to increase the green power options for local residents.

Seven states – California, Illinois, Massachusetts, New Jersey, Ohio, New York and Rhode Island – have CCA legislation enabling local governments to aggregate the electricity loads of residents, businesses, and municipal facilities, and control both the cost and amount of renewable energy in their energy mix.

VIEW THE FULL POLICY

• California's CCA legislation, AB 117, passed in 2002 (amended by SB 790 in 2011).

RESOURCES

• City Power Play: 8 Practical Local Energy Policies to Boost the Economy: community-wealth.org/sites/clone.community-wealth.org/files/downloads/City-Power-Play-8-Practical-Local-Energy-Policies-to-Boost-the-Economy.pdf

6

LAND

Open spaces are key to the health and vitality of cities. Walkable, safe, green, spaces increase the possibilities for people to meet and nurture relationships, become family, friends, and colleagues. But a discussion about Sharing Cities can't focus on open spaces alone. Gentrification should be a part of that discussion. If we, promoters of Sharing Cities, don't manage to address the tension of gentrification by having strategies to secure the livelihoods of the people who produce the urban commons and to disarm profit-maximizing interests, then the tragedy of the urban commons will only be reinforced. The way the sharing economy discourse was co-opted by profit-oriented platforms shows how quickly Sharing Cities could fall over the barrier and become just another way to reproduce existing patterns of domination.

There are groups actively working to avoid this. For example, activists of 596 Acres use data through collaborative mapping to leverage intensive grassroots organizing in support of people from poor neighborhoods of New York City, to reclaim and secure the use of vacant public land for community purposes. In Berlin, citizens managed to convene a popular vote that derailed the local government's plans to transform the former city airport in a new neighborhood by guaranteeing public ownership. In Montreuil, a quickly gentrifying city in direct periphery of Paris, an annual cultural event called the "Festival des Murs à Pêches" has been instrumental in safeguarding against development of an iconic heritage site. On another continent, a very similar strategy has been deployed by the activists of the Mukuru Festival in Nairobi, Kenya. There, a cultural event is used to transform the vision people both inside and outside the slum have of the place, empowering dwellers to create a community together.

Social capital is shaped and molded by space. This same social capital is crucial in the successful self-organization of the commons, according to the late political economist Elinor Ostrom. Thus, in places where people can mobilize social capital, decades of urban planning practices are being challenged. In Ghent, with Living Street, city administrators are tapping into the collective intelligence of citizens by letting them experiment in reinventing their streets to make them carbon neutral. In Bogota, Colombia, dialogue and an enabling legal framework is turning graffiti from a problem into what's being recognized as a cultural practice that contributes to the urban fabric. This chapter shows that local collaborative states (Sharing Cities) can enable commoning practices, let the urban commons flourish, and further strengthen social capital.

Digitalization is also an opportunity: It allows people to collect and make use of data in creative ways on an unprecedented scale. This has a huge potential for the urban commons. City administrators hold large amounts of land data that is so far hard to access or use, but when it becomes open data, it can unleash bottom-up innovations as shown in New York City by 596 Acres or in many other places with initiatives such as Code for America/Germany.

Last but not least, we should not forget that practices that foster Sharing Cities may have actually been there for decades. Some of those practices may be seen as old-fashioned, but might prove useful today. At the end of the day, because cities are all about density (of population, capital, opportunities), this land chapter clearly raises and answers questions about power and ownership in cities. How can we share power to shape urban space to make more equitable cities? How much infor- mality and disobedience may be required to enable Sharing Cities? Those are unusual questions that we would like you to keep in mind in order to critically evaluate the examples we have selected.

Adrien Labaeye

St. Clements:

Activists Transform an Abandoned Hospital Into Affordable Housing

♀ London, U.K.

─────

By Anna Bergren Miller

PROBLEM

As home prices soar, cities around the world face a crisis of affordability. In London, U.K., the situation is especially acute: According to a 2016 Lloyds Bank study, the ratio of average home sales price compared to average earnings is 10-to-6. Without the means to meet monthly mortgage costs (let alone a down payment) low- and moderate-income residents are often locked out of home ownership and the opportunity to build equity. Meanwhile, land use is determined by profit maximization rather than nonmaterial factors like social inclusion and environmental sustainability.

SOLUTION

One response to this affordability crisis is the use of community land trusts. Community land trusts permanently remove land from the conventional property market and distribute long-term leases according to community priorities, thereby increasing the supply of affordable housing. London Community Land Trust (LCLT), the capital city's first such organization, originated in negotiations between the activist group now known as Citizens UK and the 2012 Olympic bid team. When the bid team suggested a pilot community land trust project, the newly-formed LCLT (until 2015,

"People are demanding more of a say about what regeneration looks like, instead of sitting back and being told what the future of their area is going to be. It's about changing the narrative of housing: building homes rather than investment units; having security and stability in a particular place, rather than being forced to move every six months; and mobilising popular support for development."

Catherine Harrington, director of the National Community Land Trust Network

Source: The Guardian

the East London Community Land Trust) worked with the Mayor of London and the Greater London Authority to incorporate community land trust housing into a scheme to redevelop St. Clements Hospital, shuttered since 2005. In fact, LCLT has secured an agreement to build at least 20 community land trust homes on the East Wick and Sweetwater neighborhood, and is supporting similar efforts in Lewisham.

RESULTS

- LCLT allocated the homes to income-qualified applicants from an original pool of 700. The homes will be sold at approximately one-third of their open market value: one-, two-, and three-bedroom homes at £130,000, £182,000, and £235,000 ($168,000, $235,000, and $304,000), respectively.

- Resale is restricted to LCLT-approved prospective buyers, with home sellers to recoup their original investment plus a portion of appreciated value as contracted with LCLT. Other community benefits include sustainable architecture, green spaces and play areas, community space in a refurbished St. Clements building, and proximity to public transit and Cemetery Park.

- The larger St. Clements project, comprising 252 new homes built by Linden Homes with JTP Architects (architect and master planner) and the Greater London Authority, has received several awards, including Overall Winner and Best Scheme in Planning at the National Housing Awards 2014.

RESOURCES

- London Community Land Trust: www.londonclt.org

- National Community Land Trust Network: cltnetwork.org

- Summary of the 2011 Comprehensive CLT survey: cltnetwork.org/wp-content/uploads/2014/01/2011-Comprehensive-CLT-Survey.pdf

596 Acres:
Reclaiming Public Land for Communities

New York, New York, U.S.

By 596 Acres

PROBLEM

Located primarily in areas of the city where low-income communities of color live today, more than a thousand vacant public lots languish behind fences, collecting garbage. One such lot was in Paula Segal's Bedford-Stuyvesant neighborhood in Brooklyn. In 2010, she began talking to her neighbors about this lot. She gathered as much information as she could find about it and called a community meeting. That meeting led to more meetings, which led to Myrtle Village Green: an active, near-ly 2-acre community space with garden beds, an outdoor movie screening area, a pumpkin patch, and an educational production and research farm. From then on, she thought, "How many more such lots are there in New York City?" She got access to city data and learned that, in 2001, 596 acres of public land were waiting for communities to transform them, and soon after, 596 Acres was born.

SOLUTION

The 596 Acres team starts by translating the data available about vacant municipal land into information that can be useful in context, using customized mapping tools. With that knowledge in hand, they put signs on the fences of vacant city-owned lots

Paula Z. Segal, attorney, adviser and founding director, 596 Acres

that say, "This land is your land," in English and Spanish, and explain which agency has control over the property. The signs also say that neighbors, together, may be able to get permission to transform the lot into a garden, park, or farm. They list the city's parcel identifier, and information about the individual property manager handling the parcel for the agency, including a phone number.

The signs also connect neighbors to an online map and organizing web-tool called LivingLotsNYC.org and to 596 Acres' staff, who steer and support residents through a bureaucratic maze in order to gain access to the space.

596 Acres takes on a supportive and advocacy role during each campaign – but residents remain the leaders. Each space, ultimately, is managed autonomously, transformed and maintained by volunteers and local community partners to gather, grow food, and play.

RESULTS

- Since 2011, neighbors have begun campaigns to transform over 200 sites.

- 596 Acres has steered groups through the process of creating new community organizations and helped these organizations get formal access to vacant lots to create 39 new community-managed spaces.

- Nearly all of them have become so valuable to their local and citywide communities that they have been permanently preserved as community spaces by the New York City municipal government. This strategy for activating the potential of vacant public land has been emulated in over a dozen cities around the globe, including Philadelphia and Melbourne.

RESOURCES

- 596 Acres: 596acres.org

- Open-source version of the digital tool used by 596 Acres: github.com/596acres/django-livinglots

Murs à pêches à Montreuil. Photographer: Patrick Charpiat. Source:https://commons.wikimedia.org/wiki/File:Murp%C3%AAche1.JPG. Usage Rights: CC BY-SA 2.5

Les Murs à Pêches:
Leveraging Culture and Advocacy to Safeguard a Unique Landscape
Montreuil, France

By Adrien Labaeye

PROBLEM

Les Murs à Pêches is a maze of walled gardens stretching over 35 hectares (around 86.5 acres) in Montreuil, in the middle of the Paris megalopolis. This site was established five centuries ago and developed over time, as residents found out they could grow peaches because of the microclimate generated by a network of walls that accumulate heat during the day and release it at night.

Over the course of the last century, the commercial culture of the fruit declined, and many walls began to slowly crumble. In 1994, the whole place was rezoned and 80 percent of the area was open for urbanization, putting at risk this unique horticultural heritage and opening the door to the privatization of land that was publicly owned. What was the best way to encourage city dwellers and the government to value and preserve Les Murs à Pêches?

SOLUTION

A nonprofit association called M.A.P. was formed in 1994 to advocate for the preservation of the site. Initially, the group wanted the whole site to be protected from

"Here the walls do not separate
lots, they are built in the middle.
They were built to create [a
microclimate]."

Hugo, member of the Federation des Murs à Pêches

developers. In order to increase the visibility of this unique site, local associations organized a multicultural festival.

As the result of this bottom-up mobilization, in 2003, the French government issued a decree to protect 8.5 hectares of the Mûrs à Pêches. A handful of cultural associations obtained concessions to use garden lots, opening them to the public. These associations, federated within the "Fédération des Murs à Pêches," organize a cultural festival every year as a strategic effort to build a strong network of citizens who are ready to oppose future urbanization of the site. A second crucial element of the festival is to bring the distinct populations that form the city of Montreuil together, to reinforce social cohesion.

RESULTS
- The planned residential and mixed areas were not developed. Most of the 35 hectares remain, and 8.5 hectares (21 acres) are protected area.
- More than 20 nonprofit organizations are involved in preserving the site.
- Many walls have been restored by M.A.P. using traditional building techniques through volunteer action and public funding.
- The Festival des Murs à Pêches has been held for 16 consecutive years and has brought together more than 3,000 participants to the space.

RESOURCES
- Federation des Murs à Pêches (French): federationmursapeches.jimdo.com

Bottom Road Sanctuary:
A Post-Apartheid Community Managed Nature Sanctuary

Cape Town, South Africa

By Adrien Labaeye

The area around Zeekoevlei lake, in South Africa, has had extremely high concentrations of threatened native plant species. This is partly because its northern bank was used as a garbage dump for many years. Then, in 2005, the city of Cape Town rezoned the area into parcels of land to be purchased by people who suffered through the Apartheid. The residents who moved in joined forces with nature conservation officials and local environmental organizations to restore the wetland. In practice, this meant residents largely left the space open and undeveloped. Some residents have actively removed invasive species, allowing a particularly threatened plant species, the fynbos, to thrive again in its natural habitat. The Bottom Road Sanctuary now has over 50,000 native plants, attracting many kinds of wildlife. It also has walkways, benches, and barbecuing spaces for nearby residents to share.

RESOURCES

• Bottom Road Sanctuary: bottomroadsanctuary.co.za/about

Gängeviertel:
Repurposed Historical Building for Public Art and Culture

⊙ Hamburg, Germany

By Adrien Labaeye

LAND

The city of Hamburg decided to tear down a deteriorating historical building complex in a neighborhood once known as "das Gängeviertel." In August 2009, artists formed a collective to oppose the destruction of the 12 buildings, and advocated that they instead be repurposed as a public space for creativity. The collective succeeded in saving the Gängeviertel, and held a launch celebration. The event brought 3,000 residents of Hamburg into the space for exhibitions, film screenings, concerts, and other cultural events. The collective then transformed into a co-operative in 2010, and presented a concept plan for the complex to the local urban development authority in Hamburg. The city approved the plan and granted the co-op's use and management of the buildings. In the six years since, several of the buildings have been renovated by the city and tens of thousands of people have visited the cultural complex. In 2012, the German UNESCO Commission celebrated the Gängeviertel initiative as a successful example of urban development that promotes cultural and social participation through the preservation of public spaces and democratic city policies.

RESOURCES
• Gängeviertel (German): das-gaengeviertel.info

Chişinău Civic Center:
Vacant Lot Reclaimed as a Public Park for Community Gatherings

Chişinău, Moldova

By Cat Johnson

A neglected plot of triangular land once lay in the city of Chişinău. Cars regularly drove over it. Some used it to dump their garbage and construction rubble. Now, the site is a lively public space, known as the Chişinău Civic Center. The transformation was initiated by the local nongovernmental organization the Oberliht Association, and was created together with local officials as well as artists, architects, scientists, students, and community members. In the very beginning, they held a public picnic at the park as a way to invite nearby residents to get involved in the park's restoration. The organizers then built a wooden platform in the center of the park with support of the nearby residents. This eventually led to the Civic Center becoming a play area for children, as well as a place for community gatherings, film screenings, games, exhibits, and performances.

RESOURCES
- About the SPACES Public Program: "Chişinău Civic Center – beyond the red lines": http://www.spacesproject.net/images/doku/aboutspacespublicprogrammechisinau.pdf

"

THE ONLY THING THAT WILL REDEEM MANKIND IS COOPERATION.

– BERTRAND RUSSELL

Champlain Housing Trust, One of Over 250 Community Land Trusts in the U.S. Creating Permanently Affordable Housing

Burlington, Vermont, U.S.

By Anna Bergren Miller

Community Land Trusts (CLTs) are nonprofit entities dedicated to maintaining community control of real property outside conventional, speculative land and housing markets. Though they may serve other ends – including the stewardship of green space or agricultural land – CLTs are typically designed around the provision of permanently affordable housing for low-income individuals and families.

The features of CLTs vary by country. However, many are patterned after the original United States model and have the following features in common. The central feature is that CLTs separate ownership of land and houses. CLT's allow residents to buy a house while securing a long-term lease on the underlying land from the CLT. While the trust is typically organized as a nonprofit steered by a board of directors comprised of CLT homeowners, area residents, and other stakeholders, it maintains permanent ownership of the land while the homeowner owns the house and any improvements to it.

Resale of the house is restricted to CLT-approved buyers. In addition to the principal investment and the value of improvements, the house seller recoups a limited portion of the house's appreciation on terms contracted in advance with the CLT. This setup protects CLT housing from appreciation typical of housing markets to ensure at least some permanently affordable housing for the community.

The CLT concept was developed by Robert Swann, who was in turn inspired by Ralph Borsodi. Swann and Borsodi shared an interest in the Indian "Gramdan," or village gift movement. Other historical precursors including Native American land-use practices and the New England commons. In partnership with Slater King, Martin Luther King Jr.'s cousin, Swann established the first CLT in the U.S. in Albany, Georgia. New Communities Inc. was explicitly modeled on the Jewish National Fund's Israel land-lease policy.

Although growing, the worldwide CLT movement remains relatively small. Nonetheless, a 2011 survey identified nearly 250 CLTs in the U.S. alone. CLTs are also active in several other countries including Belgium, France, Italy, Kenya, Australia, New Zealand, and England.

Vermont's Champlain Housing Trust (CHT) is the largest CLT in the United States. Founded in 1984 as two separate nonprofit organizations that merged in 2006, CHT operates in three counties and oversees 565 owner-occupied homes plus 2,200 rental apartments. The trust offers other services – including homeowner education, home improvement and energy efficiency loans, and assistance – to five housing cooperatives.

CHT's shared equity program sells homes on trust-owned land to prospective homeowners who meet certain income and asset requirements. Homebuyers pay closing costs of $6,000-8,000, but the down payment (20-30 percent of market value) is covered by state and federal grants. Upon resale, CHT home-owners receive their original contribution plus 25 percent of any appreciation. In 2015, 44 new CHT residents purchased homes at an average CHT net price of $137,214, for an average CHT monthly cost of $994.78.

Because CLTs are effective in expanding affordable housing, cities are increasingly supporting them in various ways, including policy.

VIEW A REPORT ON CLT POLICIES
- http://www.lincolninst.edu/publications/policy-focus-reports/city-clt-partnership

RESOURCES
- National Community Land Trust Network: cltnetwork.org

- 2011 CLT survey: http://cltnetwork.org/wp-content/uploads/2014/01/2011-Comprehensive-CLT-Survey.pdf

- Shareable article: www.shareable.net/blog/how-to-start-a-community-land-trust

New Residential Zoning Allows Peer-to-Peer Rental of Parking Spaces, Storage Areas, and Gardens

Montréal, Canada

By Maira Sutton

The Rosemont–La Petite-Patrie borough of Montréal, Canada, modified its by-laws to allow its residents and property owners to earn money for the use of their parking spaces by other individuals. The by-laws regulate peer-to-peer rental of driveways for parking, as well as homes and garages for storage, and yards for gardening. Previous restrictions prohibited such commercial activities in residential areas. The new regulations optimize the use of existing, privately-owned spaces through shared use.

The neighborhood, which is a hip commercial area with high-traffic health facilities, has lacked adequate parking for several years. Meanwhile, hundreds of driveways of nearby residences lay vacant during the day. The by-laws were modified to allow these private parking spaces to be rented out in order to offset the need to build new parking structures.

The new policies also permit the rental of yards for community gardening, which is growing increasingly popular in the area. People that want to grow vegetables or flowers are now able to rent land directly from neighbors. The by-laws were also modified to allow the rental of spaces in homes and garages for storage.

Officials representing the area passed these rules out of a commitment to modernizing their city through shared use, which they saw as a pragmatic solution to growing resource constraints. They were determined to enable these new uses in the simplest way possible, and did so by clarifying existing regulations, rather than drafting new policies from scratch. The by-laws were also modified to deter corporations from capitalizing on these spaces. For example, the spaces for storage or gardening may not exceed mandated sizes, and shops may not rent from residences to store merchandise.

VIEW THE FULL POLICY

- (French) drive.google.com/drive/folders/0B7QZ6oJxCT4kZEpiaE9xelYzbjg

RESOURCES

- News story on the new policy (French): www.ledevoir.com/societe/actualites-en-societe/469556/rosemont-ouvre-la-voie-au-airbnb-du-stationnement

Rotterdam's Policy for Open Land Data

Rotterdam, Netherlands

By Adrien Labaeye, based on materials provided by Rob Poll-van Dasselaar and Joris Goos *(city of Rotterdam)*

Data about land is a highly coveted resource in most cities. Indeed, knowing the characteristics of a given lot, its value, its ownership, and its risk exposure provides strategic information for urban planners, investors, and citizens. Too often, this data is managed as a bounty by local public administrators who restrict access. This certainly hinders transparency and generally the sharing of information, even among local government agencies themselves. Preceding national policy (2011), however, the city of Rotterdam has elected to explore the application of open data principles to land policy. Over 500 geospatial datasets are open. Some are open by national law, such as large scale topography and building information, but many additional datasets have been opened by the forward-looking local administration, including aerial photos, 3D city models, underground infrastructure such as cables and pipelines, and more. This policy is rooted in the understanding that open data enables collaboration across agencies in the city. This is seen as instrumental to achieving a municipal vision of becoming a smart and resilient city ready for the next economy.

The policy, in a nutshell:

- All datasets, except geospatial ones, are available on one single platform for open data: http://rotterdamopendata.nl.

- A systematic review of datasets is undertaken before they are uploaded to the Open Data Store. Aspects such as privacy, data formats, and more are considered.

- A public-private partnership is being created to improve the Open Data Store of Rotterdam.

- The impact of the policy is not yet measured, which could be addressed by the public-private partnership

VIEW THE FULL POLICY

- (Dutch) www.persberichtenrotterdam.nl/uploads/Voorjaarsnota%20 2016%20-%202020%20def.pdf

Intersection Repair to Create Safer Streets

♀ Portland, Oregon, U.S.

By Cat Johnson

City streets, even in residential neighborhoods, are generally designed exclusively for cars. This shift of focus from pedestrians, cyclists and other nonmotorized means of transport can lead to dangerous situations. In 1996, in Portland, Oregon, two young girls were struck and killed by a car while crossing the road on their way to a park.

Neighbors banded together to create a local organization named City Repair and its flagship initiative, Intersection Repair. An internationally-renowned, city-sanctioned, placemaking project, Intersection Repair helps communities transform streets and intersections into vital, human-scale public spaces by painting them, installing Little Free Libraries and other microstructures, providing areas for seating, and more.

After the success of the first Intersection Repair, which was done without permission from local officials, neighbors gathered testimonials and created a proposal to legitimize the project. The proposal was approved by the Portland Bureau of Transportation and formalized into an ordinance. The organization now has the support of the city of Portland, which gives permits to communities coordinating Intersection Repair projects in their neighborhood. As of January 2017, the Portland Bureau of Transportation has 49 completed intersection projects on record and City Repair now fields calls from people around the world hoping to learn from their experience.

VIEW THE FULL POLICY
• www.portlandoregon.gov/transportation/67083

Foreclosure Fine Ordinance

Richmond, California, U.S.

By Maira Sutton

Cities across the U.S. experienced a record number of foreclosures following the burst of the housing bubble in 2007 and the ensuing financial crisis. Millions of people were unable to pay their mortgages and subsequently lost their homes to banks and mortgage companies. These financial institutions were then left with the task of maintaining a large number of vacant properties, which they were not equipped to do. In order to disincentivize banks from foreclosing on occupied residences, the city of Richmond passed the Foreclosure Fine Ordinance in 2008. The ordinance established a fine on property owners, including banks, of $1,000 per day if they failed to maintain their vacant properties up to city code. The aim was to keep more people in their homes and allow them to maintain their properties. Otherwise, a large number of vacant homes would likely enter into disrepair and trigger a process of urban decay.

VIEW THE FULL POLICY
- www.ci.richmond.ca.us/1091/Vacant-Dwellings-and-Buildings

Begum Bazaar, a Self-regulating 'High-Street'

Hyderabad, India

By Adrien Labaeye

Despite car-centric urban development and top-down decision-making, the Begum Bazaar – a historic wholesale market which has existed for over 400 years – has remained a shared social space hosting a vibrant economy. The use of street space surrounding the market is appropriated by vendors through complex practices of mediation and includes a mix of formal and informal rules. Acquiring a space requires informal negotiation between neighbors, and is not always without conflict. Vendors may inherit or be granted the right to use street space through verbal agreement by other established vendors from the same geographical origin or religion. Generally, compliance with formal rules is low, but it is far from being an ungoverned space. Thus, parking is regularly used by vendors, leaving motorists without space, maximizing its value as a marketplace.

In Begum Bazaar, the regulation of street space is representative of the eight design principles of common pool resource management as outlined by Nobel Prize winning economist Elinor Ostrom in her book "Governing the Commons: The Evolution of Institutions for Collective Action." This is not a straightforward example to be replicated, but rather it showcases what self-organization can bring: a vibrant, diverse, and pedestrian-oriented space in a city where most other scenarios of top-down governance has often led to gentrification and car-centric development.

VIEW THE FULL POLICY
• Book chapter on urban commons and Begum Bazaar (page 72): goo.gl/aprddb

WASTE

Waste is an immense global problem. Cities play a key role in generating much of this waste. According to the World Bank, cities across the world produce approximately 1.3 billion tons of solid waste annually, and this is projected to increase to 2.2 billion tons by 2025. The negative side effects of the current levels of waste generation range from environmental pollution to public health crises.

Nothing is wasted in nature. Natural ecosystems absorb organisms at the end of their life cycle as nutrients that are used to feed other plants and animals. A paradigm shift is needed in city policies and community initiatives to turn waste into a useful resource. Key to this is the idea of the circular economy, an upstream solution that envisions a continuous and positive development cycle that preserves and enhances natural capital, optimizes resources, and minimizes waste generation, as per the Ellen MacArthur Foundation, an organization based in the U.K. which promotes the circular economy. The basic principle of a circular economy is that there are infinite possibilities of reusing what has already been produced. It is a way of thinking that promises to push manufacturers further in conceiving their products in entirely different ways. From a circular-economy perspective, materials and products are created to eventually become something else. Waste is reconceived as a resource and not as something to be thrown away.

Zero waste is an important related theme and many cities have developed long-term strategies to embrace this idea. The Zero Waste International Alliance defines zero waste as a goal to "guide people in changing their lifestyles and practices to emulate sustainable natural cycles, where all discarded materials are designed to become resources for others to use." One of the biggest novelties introduced in many zero-waste regulations is the recognition of waste prevention as the area with the biggest potential. In fact, turning the traditional waste hierarchy pyramid on its head and prioritizing prevention is one the biggest successes of the diffusion of the zero-waste approach.

When cities formulate waste policies they often fail to factor in the potential for grassroots initiatives and the positive participation of local communities. It is important for cities to be bold in their support of community-led solutions and allocate budgets towards initiatives that can demonstrate a track record of success. Recognition and policy support for food waste reduction, community composting, the repair movement, and other waste prevention solutions can bring together a more diverse group of stakeholders to achieve collective impact. This has the potential to move cities along a different trajectory where zero waste and resource recovery and prevention become the key priorities. This requires a new social contract between cities, citizens, and state and local institutions that is based on mutual trust, innovative thinking, and open participation to achieve shared goals.

This chapter profiles a number of leading global case studies and policies that demonstrate how social innovation, infrastructure provision, behavior change campaigns, and supportive regulatory mechanisms can put our cities on the path toward a zero-waste future. Common features include legal structures that encourage commons-oriented solutions for mutual benefit that are inclusive in their efforts to promote community participation. The stakeholders involved vary – from citizens to grassroots organizations, all the way up to national governments. Waste reduction requires innovation at a whole systems level. The policies and case studies assembled here encapsulate the promise of new collaborative urban approaches to addressing the problem of waste through a convergence of top-down and grassroots interventions where it makes sense to do so. As the examples demonstrate, governments, worker cooperatives, social enterprises, and communities can collaborate to create impactful Sharing City solutions through technical and social innovations that sustain positive outcomes for people and the environment.

Darren Sharp and Marco Quaglia

Madeleine Froncek with compost trailer. Photographer: Compost Pedallers. Source: Compost Pedallers. Usage Rights: Fair Use Non Commercial No Derivatives

Compost Pedallers Turn Food Waste Into a Boon for Local Communities

Austin, Texas, U.S.

By Darren Sharp

PROBLEM

Around the world, 1.3 billion tons of food is wasted each year – an estimated one-third of the world's food supply, according to the Food and Agriculture Organization of the United Nations. This not only causes significant economic losses, but also has detrimental impacts on the environment. Food waste occurs not only on the industrial level, but also at restaurants and households every single day. A significant amount of food waste finds its way into landfills, producing vast amounts of methane, a highly potent greenhouse gas that contributes to global warming. Meanwhile, there is growing demand for organic compost from community gardens and urban farms. It's a complex, global challenge. How can we address it on the local level?

SOLUTION

One organization is tackling the problem head-on by taking discarded food and turning it into a beneficial resource for local communities. Compost Pedallers is a 100 percent bike-powered compost recycling enterprise in Austin, Texas, that collects compostable organic waste from homes and businesses and takes it to local urban farms and community gardens. This integrated approach reduces food waste and creates compost for urban agriculture, which strengthens local food systems and fosters social connectedness at the neighborhood level.

The group's fleet of cargo bikes are outfitted with three 32-gallon bins. Each bike can carry 500-800 pounds of food waste. Pedallers engage the community by polling neighborhood residents to determine which areas they should serve. The organization also has a rewards program called "The Loop," which lets composters earn points that can be redeemed at local businesses for seasonal produce, drinks, and yoga classes.

RESULTS

- In 2012, Compost Pedallers started its inaugural compost collection from just over 30 residential homes in Austin's Cherrywood neighborhood. According to chief executive officer and founder Dustin Fedako, Compost Pedallers now serves more than 600 residential members and 30 commercial members, and has turned over 700,000 pounds of organic waste into compost. Residential members pay $16 per month and commercial members pay between $30-$200 each month.

- According to the organization's website, "biking keeps the resources local, creates local jobs, eliminates fossil fuels and maximizes efficiency." By using the cargo bikes, the group has saved more than 55,000 gallons of fuel since 2012 and over 4 million calories have been expended from pedallers creating healthy citizens and environment.

- Grassroots solutions can be very context-specific; just because a solution works in one community doesn't mean it will be applicable in another. While Compost Pedallers cargo bikes have successfully diverted nearly 1 million pounds of organics, one should take into account the density of pickup and drop-off points, terrain, bike lane infrastructure, and cultural perception of cycling before implementing a bicycle-based service.

RESOURCES

- Compost Pedallers: compostpedallers.com

- Food and Agriculture Organization of the United Nations: www.fao.org/save-food/resources/keyfindings/en

Curitiba Green Exchange Program Uses Waste to Offer a Path out of Poverty

⚲ Curitiba, Brazil

By Darren Sharp and Marco Quaglia

PROBLEM

Cities in developing countries often lack funding for waste-management facilities that are equipped to recycle organic and nonorganic waste. This lack of infrastructure exposes many economically marginalized communities to pollution and creates a downward spiral of environmental and health problems. Food security is also a major issue for people living in these communities. This results in higher levels of malnutrition. For those living in slums, access to public transportation is often limited and expensive, which leads to further social and economic exclusion.

SOLUTION

Back in 1989, the Curitiba "Cambio Verde" (Green Exchange), was one of several interconnected city programs that was created in response to a national policy that recognized solid waste as a vehicle to eliminate poverty. The core of these programs was to shift the paradigm from viewing waste as a problem to seeing it as an economic resource.

The Green Exchange program encapsulates this approach by encouraging people living in slums to collect organic and recyclable waste, separate it, and deposit it

> "Garbage removal is a citizen responsibility. I was looking at our collection system and just realized it had to be a curbside pick up system and we went from there. Many cities make things complicated that shouldn't be complicated."

Curitiba's former Mayor Jaime Lerner

Source: Huffington Post

at the nearest waste stations. In exchange for this work, people receive food, bus tickets, school books, and other useful items. The exchange is carried out fortnightly in various areas around the city of Curitiba, based on a calendar managed by the city's environmental department.

RESULTS

- The Curitiba Green Exchange's innovative solution has helped remove waste from slums and surrounding areas, increased awareness on waste, and has unlocked an even broader range of social and economic benefits. The program, with a strong sustainable development agenda through education on environmental preservation, combats hunger, malnutrition, and poverty by giving people the opportunity to exchange waste for food.

- It has also generated a number of employment opportunities, because the city's poorest residents could now travel to the city center for work. These employment opportunities bring in more tax revenue to fund public services – so the city benefits, too.

- Green Exchange employs around 600 workers, and Curitiba is now one of the most successful cities globally in waste management. In 2010, the program won the Globe Sustainable City Award for excellence in sustainable urban development.

RESOURCES

- Cambio Verde (Portuguese):
  www.curitiba.pr.gov.br/conteudo/cambio-verde-smab/246

The Repair Café Foundation Builds Community By Fixing Things

♀ Worldwide

By Darren Sharp

PROBLEM

Changing people's behavior on waste reduction and prevention is a major challenge. Too many useful products like clothing, textiles, toys, bicycles, furniture, and household appliances are discarded as waste because people lack the practical knowledge or tools to repair broken items. While some of these goods are recycled, many are thrown in landfills. Yet in numerous communities, there are people who have the knowledge and skills to bring broken stuff back to life. So how can we create a system in which their skills can be shared?

SOLUTION

In 2009, Martine Postma organized the very first Repair Café in Amsterdam, Netherlands, to do something good for the environment and build social contacts within local communities. The Repair Café connected people who were skilled in fixing things with community members who needed items to be fixed once a month at a convenient neighborhood location. The repair experts shared their knowledge with the community members, who learned that repair is possible, and often not that difficult, with a little bit of community support. People got to experience firsthand the value of repairing things instead of buying new stuff to replace them.

"Apart from this environmental impact, there is a strong social impact. Repair Café brings people together, lets you see you neighbor in a new light."

Martine Postma, founder of Repair Café Foundation

RESULTS

- "There are now over 1,000 Repair Café groups operating in 25 countries around the world," says Postma, founder of the Repair Café Foundation. "On average, groups meet once a month at which around 25 repairs are made with a 70 percent success rate. 18,000 products are repaired each month under the Repair Café International umbrella, which equates to over 200,000 products per year. If one product weighs 1 kg [or 2.2 pounds], then Repair Café groups prevent 200,000 kgs [over 440,000 pounds/220 tons] of CO_2 from being emitted each year."

- At first, the Repair Café Foundation's starter kit, which gives a blueprint on starting a repair cafe, was entirely free; but to keep the organization sustainable, the foundation needed to raise some income. The Starter Kit is now supplied via a webshop where it can be bought for a voluntary donation. Making this shift was a challenge for the foundation, but most people have been willing to pay a small sum for the kit. Organizations that promote volunteer activities need to maintain ongoing sources of revenue and the Starter Kit is a good way to cover some of the costs.

- The Repair Café Foundation has also developed close partnerships with organizations and companies that provide benefits like product discounts to local organizers and give yearly financial donations to the organization.

RESOURCES

- Repair Cafe Foundation: repaircafe.org/en/start

Stop Wasting Food:

A Consumer-led Movement to Reduce Residential and Commercial Food Waste

⚐ Multiple Locations, Denmark

By Darren Sharp

The Danish Stop Wasting Food movement ("Stop Spild Af Mad") has grown from a small Facebook group, started in 2008, to becoming the country's largest nonprofit consumer movement against food waste. Set up by consumers, for consumers, Stop Wasting Food is a nongovernmental organization that has constructively shaped public opinion in its drive to prevent food waste. It seeks to increase public awareness and decrease food waste by organizing campaigns, mobilizing the media, and encouraging discussion, debate, and public events. Stop Wasting Food is empowering consumers to take action and launch individual initiatives, such as using leftovers, shopping prudently, and donating surplus food to homeless shelters.

The movement inspired the Danish retail chain Rema 1000 to drop quantity discounts in all its local chain stores. It also led to the wide adoption of doggybags to be made available for customers to take away leftover food in Danish restaurants. The country's biggest retail chain, Coop, signed the Food Waste Manifesto – a pledge to reduce food waste in all its stores by 10 percent over a two-year period. Denmark's food waste has fallen by 25 percent since 2010, the largest reduction of any country in the EU.

RESOURCES

- Danish Stop Wasting Food movement ("Stop Spild Af Mad"): www.stopspildafmad.dk/inenglish.html

- CPH Post Online article: cphpost.dk/news/food-waste-in-denmark-down-by-25-percent.html

- Think.Eat.Save campaign website: www.thinkeatsave.org/index.php/component/content/article/78-blogs/259-let-s-be-united-against-food-waste

Resource Work Cooperative:
A Worker-owned Recycling Cooperative

◊ Hobart, Tasmania, Australia

By Darren Sharp

Resource Work Cooperative is a nonprofit, self-funding worker's cooperative based in Hobart, Tasmania. Resource has a number of business arms that support its goals of reducing waste, creating jobs, and promoting waste minimization in the community. It has been running since 1993, and now employs around 30 people – all of whom are in charge of governing and operating the business. Profits are spent on creating new jobs, investing in the cooperative's future, and donating to worthy causes. Their Tip Shop sells reusable and recycled goods directly salvaged from the nearby waste dump, from which they gather materials four or five times each day. The Community Pick Up Service provides a free collection service from residential and commercial areas to reclaim more reusable goods. Art From Trash is a popular annual exhibition of art that is produced from discarded materials. Finally, the Reuse Education project provides engaging, practical workshops for people of all ages, demonstrating the limitless potential of creative reuse and recycling.

RESOURCES
• Resource Work Cooperative: www.resource.coop

Warp It Reuse Network:
Software Enabling Interorganizational Marketplace for Office Supplies

◊ Various Locations, Australia, Canada, U.K., and U.S.

By Darren Sharp

As organizations grow in size, it becomes challenging to determine opportunities for staff to shift surplus items around to meet equipment needs, so what often happens is new goods are bought and old goods are thrown out needlessly. Warp It Reuse Network is a software service that creates internal marketplaces within organizations to make it easy for staff to get, give, and loan surplus stationery, furniture, and other equipment. Internal marketplaces can "friend" each other and trade assets across organizational boundaries, reducing waste and procurement demand. This creates a regionwide network where the life span of goods is extended and new purchases are reduced. In the U.K., Warp It is used by over 50 percent of universities, 20 percent of health care, 30 percent of city councils, and 50 percent of Central Government Departments. Due to its success, it has also been launched in the U.S. and Australia.

RESOURCES
• Warp It Reuse Network: www.warp-it.co.uk

"
MANY HANDS MAKE LIGHT WORK.

– JOHN HEYWOOD

Johannesburg, South Africa's Community-oriented Plan for Waste Management

♀ Johannesburg, South Africa

By Marco Quaglia

The city of Johannesburg adopted its Integrated Waste Management Plan (IWMP) and policy in 2011. The plan and related policy represents one of Africa's most comprehensive regulatory and programmatic waste-management efforts. The plan's origin stems from the national government's Waste Act of 2008, which required municipalities to develop IWMPs. Johannesburg's plan promotes an integrated approach to waste building on well-known concepts such as the waste hierarchy, cradle-to-cradle design, separation at source, and community-level proximity. The plan and Pikitup's (Johannesburg's city-owned waste management company) annual report detail many community-oriented waste-reduction activities, including environmental awards to promote waste minimization and recycling; cleanup campaigns and other educational programs targeted to certain groups (for instance, the annual provincial Cleanest Town Competition); creation of new waste cooperatives and community food gardens; and the use of performance arts and exhibitions to communicate positive messages about waste management. While progress in waste reduction is uneven, Johannesburg's participatory, community-oriented waste-management activities are worth emulating.

VIEW THE FULL POLICY
- drive.google.com/open?id=0B7QZ6oJxCT4kWFhiVmhzNDc3ekU

RESOURCES
- Pikitup's 2015 annual report: www.pikitup.co.za/wp-content/uploads/2015/08/Pikitup-Johannesburg-SOC-LTD-Annual-Report-2014-2015.pdf

Capannori's Zero-waste Strategy Includes a Municipal Reuse Center

📍 Capannori, Italy

By Marco Quaglia

The city council of Capannori adopted its zero-waste strategy in 2007. The first article sets out the ambitious goals: achieve a recycling rate of 75 percent by 2011 and zero waste by 2020. Using what experts call the "waste hierarchy," Capannori's policy makers identified 11 high-impact tactics to reduce waste. The strategy includes everything from a door-to-door waste collection scheme to a "pay-as-you-throw" waste tariff. Two of the more innovative tactics include tax incentives for small retailers who sell products loose or on tap (food and liquids), and the operation of a municipal reuse center.

At the reuse center, slightly damaged clothes, electronic devices, toys, footwear, and more are repaired and then donated to people in need or sold at low prices. The center has also held free classes on upcycling techniques, from sewing to woodwork, since 2014. The results have been dramatic. According to a case study on Zero Waste Europe's website, the city reduced waste by 39 percent between 2004 and 2012, achieved an 82 percent recycling rate in 2013, and now hundreds of cities are following its example. As planned, most of the gains in waste reduction came from focusing on tactics high on the waste hierarchy, like prevention and reuse, rather than recycling – which is low on the hierarchy.

VIEW THE FULL POLICY

• (Italian)
www.comune.capannori.lu.it/sites/default/files/urp/deliberarifiuti0.pdf

RESOURCES

• Case study about Capannori's zero-waste strategy: www.zerowasteeurope.eu/2013/09/the-story-of-capannori-a-zero-waste-champion

Melbourne's Waste Management Strategy Includes Shared Garbage Compactors and Recycling Hubs

♀ Melbourne, Australia

By Marco Quaglia and Darren Sharp

Melbourne's waste is managed within a complex set of state- and city-level plans. The city of Melbourne's Waste and Resource Recovery Plan 2015-2018 aims to reduce waste, maximize resource recovery and improve local amenity in Melbourne. The city's comparatively low diversion of municipal waste from landfill, relative to other metropolitan councils, is a key driver of the plan.

The plan supports projects that are often community designed, commons based, and publicly audited. According to the plan posted on the city of Melbourne website, 10 initiatives are being pursued during the 2015-2018 period. Initiatives include shared garbage compactors and minirecycling hubs in four waste hotspots in the city, a system where residents can earn points for recycling that can be used to buy local products, and a resident/city/building-owner collaboration to increase recycling in high-rise apartments. This plan represents a model for intelligent spending and collaborative action to reduce waste at the city level.

VIEW THE FULL POLICY

- www.melbourne.vic.gov.au/SiteCollectionDocuments/waste-and-resource-recovery-plan.pdf

RESOURCES

- Video about Melbourne waste and recycling programs: www.melbourne.vic.gov.au/business/permits-and-approvals/waste-recycling/pages/central-city-waste-and-recycling-programs.aspx

Zero Waste Citizen Challenge

◊ Roubaix, France

By Marco Quaglia

With an annual average of 243 kg (over 535 pounds) of waste per capita, citizens of Rubaix, in the north of France, were producing less than half their country's average Municipal Solid Waste (MSW). Yet their aim to reduce it even further has brought about the Zero Waste Challenge.

Despite having no executive power on separate collection and other waste-related activities, the city has started a program to lead the zero waste movement in France. The initiative challenges around one hundred volunteer families to reduce the amount of solid waste produced at household level by 50 percent over the course of a year. Offering support through an array of events like workshops, coaching initiatives, and other activities such as food exchanges, the program gives no directions – only suggestions. Interestingly, the program bypasses any intermediaries, therefore creating a direct channel between the city and the families taking part.

After the first year, results were more than encouraging, with 70 percent of participating families having reduced their waste production by around 40 percent, while 25 percent of them had achieved an 80 percent reduction. Currently in its third "season," the policy is now also replicated to target other actors such as public offices, four schools, and shopkeepers in the urban area of Roubaix.

RESOURCES
• Program details (French): www.roubaixzerodechet.fr

Waste Reduction:
An Open-Source Tool for Waste Benchmarking
♀ Helsinki, Finland

By Marco Quaglia

As Eurostat data captured from the mid-90s onwards reveals, Municipal Solid Waste (MSW) had continued to steadily increase in the EU. This increase led to prioritizing the development of policies focused on waste prevention. Petra, an open-source tool available on the Helsinki Regional Environmental Services Authority website, aims to promote waste prevention in the whole metropolitan area of Helsinki. Mainly directed at companies and local administrations, Petra's waste benchmarking allows them to monitor the overall amount of waste they produce – and therefore find the best solutions to prevent it – in line with the number of employees, turnover rate, and material consumption at each workplace. The interesting aspect of this policy is that it promotes quantitative instruments to the public and fosters the creation of networks at both private and public level to save more.

Benchmarking is available free of charge and open to any company or organization in the Helsinki, Vantaa, Espoo, Kauniainen, Kirkkonummi, and Turku areas. To further encourage companies to monitor their waste, every other year the city of Helsinki holds a ceremony to reward the most successful companies in waste reduction. With the help of this and other initiatives, Finland's MSW had reduced to 500 kg (over 1,100 pounds) per capita by 2015, down from 521 kg (1,148 pounds) in 2008.

RESOURCES
• Waste Benchmarking Helsinki:
  www.crrconference.org/Previous_conferences/downloads/hahtala.pdf

• The 2030 Strategy: www.hsy.fi/sites/Esitteet/EsitteetKatalogi/Raportit/Helsinki_
  Metropolitan_Area_Climate_strategy_summary.pdf

Reducing Event Waste:
The Zero Waste Party Pack

♀ Palo Alto, California, U.S.

By Tom Llewellyn

Disposable dishware is a popular choice when feeding large groups at parties and community events, but more often than not it generates a lot of waste. In order to curb the use of plastic, paper, and Styrofoam dishware at events, and support their zero-waste goals, the city of Palo Alto launched the Zero Waste Party Pack (ZWPP) initiative in 2012. The ZWPPs are designed to cater to a group of 24 and include a set of reusable plastic dishware, metal utensils, cloth napkins, cleaning instructions, and a durable container for transport and storage. Each set cost less than $300 to assemble and the first five years of the program have only cost the city about $20,000 – in addition to a marginal amount of staff time – with the majority of that cost going toward promotion and outreach.

The 22 "Party Packs" are distributed throughout the city and are hosted by volunteer Zero Waste Block Leaders. Any resident of Palo Alto can checkout a Party Pack by contacting a nearby block leader through the city's website.

While capturing the use data can be a difficult task, the city confirmed that in 2016 the ZWPPs were loaned out at least 162 times and were used by 4,000 people. While this is only reducing a small amount of the total waste from events in Palo Alto, they feel as if the program is equally about waste and reuse education as it is about waste diversion and prevention.

RESOURCES

- Zero Waste Party Pack Initiative: www.cityofpaloalto.org/gov/depts/pwd/zerowaste/thingstodo/party.asp#Zero%20Waste%20Party%20Pack

- Zero Waste Block Leader Program:
  www.cityofpaloalto.org/gov/depts/pwd/zerowaste/thingstodo/zwbl.asp

"

EVERYONE NEEDS HELP FROM EVERYONE.

– BERTOLT BRECHT

8

WATER

The oceans were the original global commons, fished
and navigated for ages. But new technologies have
added numerous challenges to sustaining our oceans:
offshore oil drilling, deep-sea mining, and overfishing.
However, it's crucial that water, both freshwater and
saltwater, remains a commons and held in the public
trust, because access to clean and affordable water is
a basic human right.

A widespread approach to delivering water to cities consists of establishing a municipal entity, under direct or indirect local governmental control, that collects water dues from all customers (residential as well as businesses). Water rates are determined through a political process, and are intended to provide affordable water supply and sewage treatment while covering the costs. Public water supplies of this kind are often highly successful, especially in countries where there are effective methods to keep local government accountable to its citizens. However, in some cases, municipal water utilities may become inefficient (providing a service of low quality or at high cost) if insufficient incentives are built into the system to ensure that the service is continually upgraded. In extreme cases, municipal utilities may fall seriously behind in provisioning growing cities, or may provide jobs as a form of political patronage.

One type of water distribution, beyond public and private, is a cooperative system, where the distribution system is owned by its customers. The existence of this alternative is too often ignored, but it is by no means rare. For example, in the U.S., there are over 3,000 rural water cooperatives, which were set up since the New Deal in order to cheaply build up and maintain a water supply infrastructure in the rural areas of the country.

Regardless of the ownership of a water utility (public, private, or cooperative), a utility may return polluted water to a river or the sea – especially if downriver users are not able to make an impact on decision-making. This points to the need for larger communities to assert their rights to clean water. Organizations such as Hudson Riverkeeper have developed water quality monitoring programs to hold polluters accountable as illustrated by one of the case studies.

Unfortunately, people directly affected by governing decisions about their environment, resources, and quality of life are systematically prevented from being the ones who make those decisions. Under our current systems of law and governance, those decisions are made by a central government (state or federal), and local people and their municipal governments are "preempted" (forbidden) from deciding what would best serve the creation of sustainable communities and the protection of the environment and the rights of community members.

State and federal "permitting" (legalizing) of industrial activities that harm rights and equitable access to resources like water are administered by centrally controlled regulatory bureaucracies rather than by local policies serving local needs. Decisions are preordained by state and federal laws heavily lobbied for by wealthy corporations and are carried out by regulatory agencies that are not able to respond to community priorities that conflict with corporate interests. Therefore, we need effective collective economic and political decision-making about how to use and manage water to fulfill our needs. Many nonprofits such as the Community Environmental Legal Defense Fund (CELDF) are working to protect clean water as a basic human right. CELDF has worked with numerous communities to draft Community Bills of Rights that assert legally enforceable local rights and prohibit industrial activities, even those "permitted" by state and federal law, when they violate the rights of people and nature.

Cities are at the front line, protecting access to clean water as emerging water wars unfold. In a recent report entitled "The Role of Urban Agriculture in Building Resilient Cities," authors H. DE Zeeuw et al. stated, "Rapid urbanisation generally puts high pressures on limited urban resources, like fresh water, while at the same time producing large amounts of wastewater and wastes." Cities are working to reduce risk, quantify uncertainty about having a sustainable water supply, and make communities more responsive and resilient to a changing planet.

Emily Skeehan and Nikolas Kichler

CELDF and Pittsburgh's Community Bill of Rights Banning Fracking

Pittsburgh, Pennsylvania, U.S.

By **Ben Price** *(Community Environmental Legal Defense Fund)*, **edited by Emily Skeehan**

PROBLEM

In 2010, the oil and gas industries operating in Pennsylvania were acquiring land leases that would allow them to extract natural gas using the process known as "fracking." Many rural municipalities had been targeted already for this activity, and the state Legislature had enacted laws forbidding local governments from limiting or banning the industrial activities related to fracking. The people of Pittsburgh were alarmed to learn that a few larger open spaces – and even small parcels of land in the city – had been quietly leased for fracking. The nine members of the city council were hearing from their concerned district constituents and one of the council members put out a call for advice to environmental groups, land-use law firms, and other experts. A group discussion ensued in which nearly 30 organizations participated. The overarching question raised by the council member was, "How can Pittsburgh protect its people, environment, and water supply from the toxic effects of industrial gas extraction in the city?"

SOLUTION

After hearing advice from organizations suggesting appeals to state regulatory agencies and recommendations for new local zoning laws that might limit fracking to designated "heavy industrial zones," the council member asked another important question, "Don't these proposed 'solutions' actually allow fracking, rather than stop it?" The almost unanimous answer that came back was that "it's illegal to stop the fracking, because of state preemption. The best you can do is try to limit the harm."

The Community Environmental Legal Defense Fund (CELDF) was asked for its recommendations. Rather than "regulate" the amount of harm that fracking would inflict on a city that had been cleaning up smog and brownfields for decades following the withdrawal of the steel industry, CELDF offered to draft a local civil rights law that would guarantee certain community rights, including the right to clean air, pure water, the rights of natural ecosystems to flourish, and the right to be free from toxic trespass (poisoning). The proposed city ordinance, known as a Community Bill of Rights, would protect the rights it established by banning any new industrial extraction of natural gas. Several aspects differentiated the Community Bill of Rights from proposals for regulating fracking through local land use and zoning laws. Not only did it focus on protecting fundamental rights against violation by industrial extraction of gas and recognized those rights as higher law than state administrative law, but it bypassed the entire regulatory system by asserting the authority of the city to protect said rights by exercising the right of local community self-government.

RESULTS

- In 2010, the city council of Pittsburgh, Pennsylvania, unanimously (9-0) adopted the Pittsburgh Community Bill of Rights, which created enforceable rights to clean water and air, recognized legal rights of the natural environment to exist and flourish, reaffirmed the right of local community self-government, and, in order to protect these rights, banned the extraction of natural gas using fracking and related activities.

- News of Pittsburgh's bold policy of protecting the rights of people and nature by banning fracking spread through national media and by word-of-mouth. Following Pittsburgh's legislative action, multiple other municipalities in Pennsylvania – and then in Ohio, Colorado, California, and New Mexico – drafted and adopted Community Bills of Rights. Corporate objections to adoption of the Pittsburgh measure included threats of lawsuits based on supposed violations of "corporate rights" and breach of state laws preempting local governance over corporate activities. Despite these early threats, to date there has been no litigation brought against the Pittsburgh Community Bill of Rights.

RESOURCES

- National Community Rights Network: nationalcommunityrightsnetwork.org
- Community Environmental Legal Defense Fund: www.celdf.org

Community Science Keeps Pollution in Check for the Hudson River

New York City and the Hudson Valley, New York, U.S.

By Heartie Look *(Waterkeeper Alliance)*, **edited by Emily Skeehan**

PROBLEM

Beginning at Lake Tear of the Clouds, the Hudson River cascades and winds its way through a beautiful valley for 315 miles, running alongside New York City in its last stretch before joining the Atlantic Ocean. The Hudson Valley has long been a muse for artists, a popular retreat for city dwellers, and a sanctuary for its residents, while its southern neighbor – New York City – continues to be a bustling metropolis.

However, the popularity of this region surrounding the Hudson has heightened the need to monitor the quality of its water and combat contamination flowing through increasingly overtaxed sewage systems. Although the passage of the NYS Pure Waters Bond Act and Clean Water Act – and most recently the Clean Water Infrastructure Act of 2017 – have helped protect the River's water, a lack of investment in maintenance and upgrades to sewer systems threaten the health of the river, its watershed, and the people who use it.

The U.S. Environmental Protection Agency has estimated that 3.5 million Americans are sickened each year from contact with recreational water, primarily due to pathogens associated with sewage – yet there is little government data available to define when and where waters are safe for swimming. Hudson Valley communities have proposed as many as 300 wastewater improvement projects to combat contamination, but action on those projects has been slow.

SOLUTION

To defend the health of the Hudson River and its communities, the Hudson River-keeper, a nongovernmental organization established to protect the Hudson from pollution, devised a community-led, water-quality monitoring program in which the public helps fill the vast data gap on the level of contamination and water quality problems. Unlike traditional citizen science projects – in which scientists define the problem and recruit citizens to help gather data – the organization's program began with a citizen team co-designing and leading the project with scientists from Columbia University's Lamont-Doherty Earth Observatory and Queens College, in New York. Both citizens and scientists own the results and the work.

Through the program, committed community members are trained in basic water sampling techniques to test for bacteria – indicating the presence of untreated sewage. The Hudson Riverkeeper's team and a growing number of partner labs perform these tests on a regular basis, including after heavy rainfall when contaminated runoff and other sewage leaks are heaviest. Certain scientific standards are enforced to ensure proper data collection, and all results are shared as an open-source model, meaning citizens are able to easily access and contribute to the data, empowering them to advocate for change in their own communities.

RESULTS

- This collaborative effort between citizens, organizations, and the scientific community played a significant role in the passage of New York's Sewage Pollution Right to Know Law in 2012. The law requires that untreated and partially treated sewage discharges by publicly-owned treatment works and sewer systems be reported within two hours of discovery to the New York State Department of Environmental Conservation, and within four hours to the public and municipalities.

- The law, and concerted advocacy by a coalition of organizations, has in turn been a driver of hundreds of millions of dollars in new wastewater facility investments. "In 2017, Governor Andrew Cuomo signed the Clean Water Infrastructure Act, the biggest state investment in clean water in a generation. The water quality data – and those who gather it – were a driving force behind this landmark investment," says Dan Shapley.

- With such success, the initiative has expanded within the watershed and outwards by groups such as Save the Sound in Connecticut.

RESOURCES

- Riverkeeper.org: www.riverkeeper.org/water-quality

Dutch Waterways in the shade of a Windmill. Photographer: Della Duncan.
Source: Della Duncan. Usage rights: CC BY-NC-SA 4.0

Water Management Beyond Politics

⚲ Multiple Locations, The Netherlands

By Della Duncan *(Upstream Podcast)*

PROBLEM

According to a 2012 report by the Organisation for Economic Co-operation and
Development, 40 percent of the world's population will be "living in river basins
experiencing severe water stress" by the year 2050. While most of these areas will
be responding to a reduction of both surface and groundwater, others will be dealing
with too much. The Netherlands, which has more than half of its land mass sitting
below sea level, is especially vulnerable to flooding, as climate change leads to rising
sea levels. What can be done about this?

SOLUTION

Fortunately, the Dutch have created water policies that ensure that communities
are safe and resilient despite changing conditions. They have done this by taking
the mandate of water management out of central government control and putting it
instead in the hands of "Waterschappen" – regional water governments around the
country.

In each municipality, the board members who will lead these governments are
elected every four years. These organizations then determine what their bioregion's

"More than half of the Netherlands is below sea level and without a proper water management structure, the country would be uninhabitable."

Source: Dutch Water Authorities' website

water-management needs are, covering water levels, sewage treatment, infrastructure management, water quality control, and aquatic ecosystem health. Based on the projects that must be completed, they calculate how much they will need to perform what is required of them. The water governments are supervised by the higher government (the province) to ensure that mandates are met, wage increases are fair, and project costs are reasonable. Once their budgets are approved, the public is taxed according to property ownership, with the reasoning that water management is helping to protect land and properties, and those who own more should pay more.

RESULTS

- By separating water management from the central and regional governments, the Dutch protect their relationship with water from party politics. Their work with water doesn't have to compete for a piece of the pie with education, arts, and health services and isn't at risk if a government implements austerity measures or increases military spending.

- This model has been so successful at helping them have a healthy and flourishing relationship with water that they were deemed "a global reference" by the Organization for Economic Cooperation and Development (OECD) and are advising governments around the world, including Myanmar and Indonesia, which are facing similar challenges.

- This case of localizing power, catering to bioregional needs, and caring for important work has a lot to teach us about our relationships with the commons and the natural world in general, as well as about how to create political processes to meet our complex, critical, and changing needs.

RESOURCES

- The Dutch Water Authorities: www.dutchwaterauthorities.com

- Report on the Dutch water governance model: www.uvw.nl/wp-content/uploads/2015/05/Water-Governance-The-Dutch-Water-Authority-Model-2017.pdf

Tarun Bharat Sangh:

Fostering Community-driven Solutions to Secure Water Access and Rejuvenate Rivers

Rajasthan, India

By Nikolas Kichler

India makes up around 18 percent of the global population, and yet only has access to 4 percent of the world's drinkable-water resources, according to CNN. Since the 1980s, both rural and urban areas in the country have faced drinking-water shortages and crop failures. This scarcity is exacerbated by river pollution associated with sewage disposal and industrial waste. To address this crisis, in 1985, Rajendra Singh and others formed the local nongovernmental organization Tarun Bharat Sangh (TBS, or Young India Organization) in Alvar, a rural district in Rajasthan.

TBS has worked with rural villagers to revive the use of traditional water-harvesting solutions. In particular, they used "johads" (small earthen reservoirs) to harvest rainwater in a way that reduced evaporation losses to substantially replenish local aquifers. People also shifted to organic farming techniques to make more efficient use of water. TBS advocated for these and other methods of water management as a way to bring about a culture of self-sufficiency to local farming communities. The River Arvari Parliament expanded on this objective. Following the revival of the Arvari River in 1990, representatives from the area's 72 villages formed the transparent, community-driven "river parliament" to maintain the health of the river. To date, Rajasthan communities have created and managed more than 11,000 johads, replenishing more than 250,000 wells. Within 28 years, seven river systems that had been dried up for 80 years have been revived.

RESOURCES
• Tarum Bharat Sangh: tarunbharatsangh.in

Resident Development Committees:
Community-led Management Over Local Water Supplies

Lusaka, Zambia

By Nikolas Kichler

Among the African nations, Zambia is one of the most rapidly urbanizing countries in the continent. In its capital, Lusaka, 60 percent of the population live in unplanned settlements that are an urban and rural hybrid. This has led to extensive administrative challenges over clean water and public sanitation. In response, the Lusaka Water and Sewage Company, the Lusaka City Council, and various nongovernmental organizations worked together to develop Resident Development Committees (RDCs). The RDCs provide legal entities for local residents to foster cooperation with unplanned neighborhoods, thereby allowing planning, construction, and maintenance of water utilities to become self-organized and co-managed through them. Financial responsibilities, such as fee collection, are also under their jurisdiction. Over time, the RDCs have become the primary managing units for local collective decision-making over water issues, and have sustained a regular flow of information, transparency, and accountability to the communities they represent. Many neighborhoods now have access to a reliable and largely self-sustaining source of clean water. The benefits of RDCs for unplanned communities have been so convincing that formally planned areas are also advocating for the same model.

RESOURCES

- Review of Bangalore and Lusaka case studies:
  pubs.iied.org/pdfs/10584IIED.pdf

- Paper on groundwater self-supply in Zambia: rwsnforum.files.wordpress.com/2011/11/163-groundwater-self-supply-in-peri-urban-settlements-in-zambia.pdf

- Article on Zambia's water service gap:
  dspace.lboro.ac.uk/dspace-jspui/bitstream/2134/9705/7/wama159-155.pdf

depave:
Communities Turning Pavement Into Green Public Space

Portland, Oregon, U.S.

By Eric Rosewall *(depave)* **and Adrien Labaeye**

Paved surfaces contribute to stormwater pollution, by directing rainwater with toxic urban pollutants to local streams and rivers. This, in turn, degrades water quality and natural habitats. Since Portland receives a lot of rain, impervious pavements are especially problematic for the city's stormwater management. Two friends from Portland thought of a straightforward solution to this problem: remove as much impervious pavement as possible. They organized their first official depaving event in 2008. Since then, they formed depave, a nonprofit organization that promotes the removal of pavement from urban areas to address the harmful effects of stormwater runoff, as well as to create green public spaces. depave seeks out groups that are already community-oriented, such as schools and faith-based groups, and encourages them to work together on the same project. depave has coordinated over 50 depaving projects in Portland. Eric Rosewall, depave's co-founder, reports the organization has depaved more than 12,500 square meters of asphalt since 2008, diverting an estimated 12,000 cubic meters of stormwater from storm drains. Over the years, depave has grown to support depaving across the Portland metro region and beyond, through their depave network training services.

RESOURCES
• depave: depave.org/network

"
IT IS IN THE SHELTER OF EACH OTHER THAT THE PEOPLE LIVE.

– IRISH PROVERB

Itagua's Resident-managed Sanitation Board ('Junta de Saneamiento') Provides over 50,000 Residents with Drinking Water

⚲ Itagua, Paraguay

By Nikolas Kichler

In Paraguay, 2,500 community-based "Juntas de Saneamiento" (sanitation boards) provide drinking water and/or sanitation services to members-customers. Juntas consist of a general assembly of members. The general assembly elects a board of directors that is responsible for managing services for members.

Juntas are constituted under the Law 369 of 1972 and the Decree 8910 of 1974. The start of a sanitation board is based on an act with the Ministry of Public Health and Social Welfare (SENASA). The general assembly of members, which is the highest authority within a junta, make juntas community-driven organizations. Its members self-organize and have the power to change bylaws, review the board's activities, approve investments, and elect new board members during annual meetings. The board is linked with the local government, since one of the directors must be a municipal representative selected by the mayor.

Juntas are nonprofit. They finance operations through member fees, and typically all infrastructure is owned by the junta. Expansions often rely on donors. Water quality monitoring is performed by the board.

While the junta model was originally developed for villages, the city of Itagua's junta shows that large-scale self-provision is possible. As reported in 2001 by USAID, Itagua's junta was established in 1974 and served up to 2,975 residents, the population of Itagua at the time. As of 2012, and according to a pamphlet about the junta on Fundacion Avina's website, 50 employees serve over 50,000 Itagua residents with drinking water (but no sanitation).

VIEW THE FULL POLICY
- Law 369 of 1972 (Spanish):
  www.cej.org.py/games/Leyes_por_Materia_juridica/SALUD/LEY%20369.pdf

- Law 1614 of 2000 (Spanish):
  www.erssan.gov.py/archivos/documentos/LeyN1614_9wmzj01h.pdf

RESOURCES
- Function and operation of Juntas de Saneamiento (Spanish): www.senasa.gov.py/application/
  files/3714/6066/9525/Manual-1-Organicemos-nuestra-Junta-de-Saneamiento1.pdf

- USAID report on Juntas: pdf.usaid.gov/pdf_docs/Pnack672.pdf

Hood River County Water Protection Measure

⚲ Hood River County, Oregon, U.S.

By Michael O'Heaney *(Story of Stuff)*, **edited by Emily Skeehan**

For nearly a decade, Nestlé Waters has attempted to extract and bottle water from the publicly-owned Oxbow Springs in Hood River County. The people of Hood River County defended their water by bringing together small businesses, farmers and orchardists, native people, and others to stop Nestlé. They formed a group called Local Water Alliance. The group then put together a ballot initiative that would permanently limit the amount of water that could be bottled in the county. On Tuesday, May 17, 2016, the 22,000 citizens of Hood River County passed the ballot initiative with an impressive 68 percent of the vote.

The initiative, pushed forward by a coalition of disparate actors, amends Hood River County's Charter by prohibiting commercial bottled water production in Hood River County. The Water Protection Measure (Measure 14-55) is a common-sense way to protect the local water supply for use by local families, farms, and fisheries. The Water Protection Measure will stop the production of roughly 750 million plastic bottles annually. That's an elimination of 6 percent of water bottle consumption in the United States. It also sets an important precedent for water protection across the U.S., and it builds the strength of an ever-growing movement of concerned people fighting water privatization all over the world.

The Story of Stuff community made a huge difference by supporting the creation of an online campaign video, Our Water, Our Future. The Story of Stuff Project is shifting the balance of power by bringing to light the stories of heroic citizens who are taking on Nestlé around the world. Following the passage of the county ordinance, the city of Cascade Locks challenged it claiming that city rights supersede county measures.

VIEW THE FULL POLICY

- www.co.hood-river.or.us/vertical/Sites/%7B4BB5BFDA-3709-449E-9B16-B62A0A0DD6E4%7D/uploads/Publication_14-55.pdf

RESOURCES

- Story of Stuff's campaign video: storyofstuff.org/movies/our-water-our-future

How Cochabamba's Water War Led to the Reversal of Privatization and Recognition of Self-organized Water Management in Bolivia

◌ Cochabamba, Bolivia

By **Johannes Euler** *(Das Commons Institute)*

In Cochabamba, Bolivia, the lack of water has caused conflicts for decades. In 1999, Cochabamba's public water supplier, SEMAPA, was leased to the international consortium Aguas del Tunari. The major shareholder of the consortium was the multinational company Bechtel. In the course of the privatization procedures, independent water and irrigation systems and autonomous water services were threatened with expropriation. Water prices rose steeply as a result. In response, several civil society groups formed the "Coordinadora de Defensa del Agua y de la Vida" (Coalition for the Defense of Water and Life). Protests against these policies were fierce, lasted several months, and raised the issue to national and international levels.

Eventually, Aguas del Tunari was expelled. Control of SEMAPA was transferred to representatives from the municipality, the trade union, and the Coordinadora (though these arrangements have subsequently changed). The statutes of the hybrid company were rewritten in a challenging participatory process, but SEMAPA is still known for its lack of efficiency and transparency. Moverover, the state is currently trying to extend its sphere of control into the water sector. However, the so-called Cochabamba Water War contributed to major changes in Bolivia's water sector, the respective laws, the establishment of a national Ministry of the Environment and Water, and of the country as a whole.

Key points of Bolivian policy reforms sparked by the Cochabamba Water War:

- In 2000, the pro-privatization Law 2029 was canceled and rewritten as Drinking Water and Sanitation Services Law (2066). It was the result of negotiations between social movements and the state during the water wars. It recognized marginalized communities' rights to use water and differentiated them from capitalist activities, which had to be authorized and were subject to fees.

- In 2004, similar principles were applied to the irrigation sector (Law 2878), which recognized decentralized irrigation governance. Both laws support indigenous people and farm laborers from being dispossessed of water. At the same time, they contributed to the formalization of water management, which tends to favor commercial management over community management.

- The Bolivian constitution was changed in 2009. Prior to 2009, water supply concessions could be granted for up to 40 years. The new constitution considers water a basic right of life and bans the typical methods of privatization and leasing of water services to for-profit entities. Sustainability and public participation are declared to be the responsibility of the state as well as universal access to water. To which extent these intentions will actually be reflected in reality remains to be seen, however. The responsibilities coming with this basic-rights approach demand action by the state and challenge community management at the same time.

RESOURCES

- Article on water laws in the Andes: www.researchgate.net/profile/ Maria_Cecilia_Roa-Garcia/publication/259505349_Water_laws_in_ the_Andes_A_promising_precedent_for_challenging_neoliberalism/ links/54adb9a10cf24aca1c6f6bd6.pdf

- Ph.D. thesis on community water systems in Cochabamba (Spanish): 132.248.9.195/ptd2014/marzo/507452041/Index.html

Public Platform for Citizen-led Water Management

Porto Alegre, Brazil

By Nikolas Kichler

In order to meet the rising demands of Porto Alegre's rapidly growing population during the early 1900s, the municipal government took over inefficient private water companies. The financially independent, publicly owned, autonomously operating, "Departamento Municipal de Água e Esgoto" (Municipal Water and Sewerage department, or DMAE in Portuguese) successfully developed necessary water treatments, and improved and extended the network.

Reforms following Brazil's military dictatorship (1964–1985) included citizen decision-making power over their water utilities and participatory governance mechanisms, such as the Deliberative Council and the Participatory Budgeting. These have significantly contributed towards the modern success of the DMAE.

The Deliberative Council (DC) is one of the DMAE's three functional management bodies. Formed by a heterogeneous group of experts and delegates from citizens' organisations, the DC is a non-party institution that controls and approves all operations and decisions taken by the DMAE. How the budget is spent is also decided by the people: the annual Participatory Budgeting process, whose internal rules are established by participating citizens themselves, lets them choose the priority level of upcoming city projects through neighbourhood assemblies, "thematic" assemblies, and citywide coordinating sessions.

The DMAE has become the largest and one of the most efficient municipal providers of sanitation services in Brazil. Treated water reaches 100 percent of Porto Alegre's population, and sewer collection services cover 87.7 percent. Participatory budgeting has significantly improved situations in peripheral areas, with around 50,000 residents taking part on this process.

RESOURCES

- Official DMAE website (Portuguese): www2.portoalegre.rs.gov.br/dmae

- The Case for Public Provisioning in Porto Alegre: http://citeseerx.ist.psu.edu/ viewdoc/download?doi=10.1.1.605.7570&rep=rep1&type=pdf

River Granted Full Rights of Legal Personhood

⚲ Multiple Locations, New Zealand

By Tom Llewellyn

In March 2017, the New Zealand Parliament passed the "Te Awa Tupua" (Whanganui River Claims Settlement) Bill to provision the full rights of personhood upon the Whanganui river. This landmark legislation was 140 years in the making, as the Whanganui iwi tribe had campaigned for the river to be recognised as a living entity with legal rights since the 1870s. With this new designation, if the river is harmed or contaminated it will result in the same penalties and legal ramifications as if damage or injury had been done to the tribe or any of its members, because it is now recognized as being one and the same.

Guardians from both the Whanganui iwi and the New Zealand government have been appointed to act on behalf of the river, which will be legally represented by two lawyers, and treated like a charitable trust. The legislation also provisions $80 million New Zealand dollars ($56 million) as reparations to the iwi and NZ$30 million ($21 million) toward a legal defense fund, and NZ$1 million ($700,000) to form the necessary legal framework.

Shortly after this ruling, a similar designation was given to the Ganges river by a court in India that referenced the New Zealand law as a precedent for their decision.

RESOURCES

• Te Awa Tupua Bill: http://www.legislation.govt.nz/bill/government/2016/0129/latest/DLM6830851.html?src=qs

Water Remunicipalisation From Private to Public Management

◊ Paris, France *(and worldwide)*

By Tom Llewellyn

The modern privatization of municipal water utilities began in London in the early 1990s and rapidly spread throughout the world, with the majority of cases taking place in the global South. But, with a track record of increased costs and a history of many private companies failing to deliver promised improvements to infrastructure and service reach, cities around the world have begun to push back.

Remunicipalisation of water infrastructure, provisioning, and sanitation involves a city – or other municipality – either not renewing or breaking a contract with a private company in order to return the management of these services to municipal authorities. According to the 2015 report from The Transnational Institute, "Our Public Water Future," between 2000 and 2015 there have been 235 cases of water remunicipalisation in 37 countries.

In 2008, the Paris City Council voted against renewing its contracts for the private management of the city's water system by Suez and Veolia – two of the biggest private water management companies globally – and created a new public entity, Eau De Paris, to take their place. In 2010 – the first year Eau De Paris was operating – there was 35 million euro (roughly $39 million) in savings, which lead to an 8 percent reduction in costs to consumers.

VIEW THE FULL POLICY (French)

- (French) a06.apps.paris.fr/a06/jsp/site/Portal.jsp?page=ods-solr.display_document&id_document=64507&items_per_page=20&sort_name=&sort_order=&terms=&query=&fq=seance_string%3AAVRIL%202009

RESOURCES

- Water Remunicipalisation Tracker: www.remunicipalisation.org

- PSIRU water remunicipalisation report: www.psiru.org/sites/default/files/2014-11-W-HeretoStay.pdf

- TNI publication on water remunicipalisation: www.tni.org/files/download/ourpublicwaterfuture-1.pdf

"

LIVE LIKE A
MIGHTY RIVER.

– BUDDHA

9

TECHNOLOGY

Corporate platforms enabled by Information and Communication Technologies (ICTs) are sometimes seen as exploitative and even illegal by cities. The worst offenders, like Airbnb and Uber, have been described as Death Stars that extract vast amounts of value from local communities only to transfer that wealth elsewhere, sometimes into tax havens. Indeed, it would seem that the original ideas of sharing and peer-to-peer collaboration have been co-opted through an almost feudal structure of wealth extraction. Technology as such is not the culprit here. But it certainly enables the creation of new products and markets that, in practice, can perpetuate or even deepen existing socio-economic inequities. As long as tech development is dominated by global capital and intellectual elites, it seems difficult to see how it can contribute to empower local communities.

In contrast to the usual examples of on-demand "sharing" platforms, this chapter examines initiatives and policies that demonstrate technology's capacity to enable real sharing within cities. These examples offer crucial alternatives to extractive platforms that are currently dominant. They are also solutions that are intentionally designed to address urban challenges, instead of exacerbating them. There are solutions based on an understanding of digital technology as what Ivan Illich defined as tools for conviviality: tools that empower people to realize their freedom through interpersonal dependence and reciprocity.

This chapter also demonstrates how commoning practices have the potential to enable the reappropriation and repurposing of technology. The emerging digital space is a new territory where citizens can collaboratively leverage their right to the city. For this to happen, diversity, digital literacy, civic capacity – but also supportive community places such as hackerspaces – have shown to be key ingredients.

However, we must not be mistaken that as inspiring as they are, the initiatives featured in this chapter generally fall short of fully deconstructing existing patterns of subordination based on gender, race, and class, which are particularly strong when technology is in the focus. We acknowledge, and are cognizant of, this fact. These ideas however, are replicable and improvable. We hope that others will – like free and open-source lines of code – fork, improve, and release their own solutions that will more fully realize the emancipatory potential of technology. This very book, licensed under a Creative Commons Attribution license, attempts to recursively promote those ideas that are easy to reproduce.

Adrien Labaeye and Ryan T. Conway

Students at Bloomington Code School learn from a volunteer lecturer. Photographer: Katie Birge. Source: Bloomington Code School. Usage rights: CC BY-NC-SA 4.0

Bloomington Creates Shareable Information and Communication Technologies

♀ Bloomington, Indiana, U.S.

By Ryan T. Conway

PROBLEM

In 2005, officials from the city of Bloomington and Indiana University saw that a budding tech sector could be the future of the city. The university's School of Informatics had just acquired its own buildings, with a forthcoming deal to house the department of computer science.

Meanwhile, the State of Indiana had approved Bloomington's application for a 65-acre Certified Technology Park, allowing the city to keep some CTP tax revenues and prompting it to court new technology firms.

Beyond business and research, Bloomington had a growing tech culture. Humanetrix, a nonprofit organization founded in 2002 that supports technologists' public interest projects, had already launched three major tech and innovation events by 2011: The Combine, Ignite Bloomington, and TedXBloomington. Adding to the scene, 2010 saw the birth of Bloomington's first hackerspace, Bloominglabs, which hosts free, weekly open nights, and the launch of an annual Makevention event, drawing dozens of exhibitors and hundreds of area residents. What's a good way to ensure that people are empowered to share in Indiana's growing tech sector?

"Community coding programs are exciting because you can scale them to the size of your community but they truly are community efforts and you need community backing to get them up and running."

<u>Katie Birge, founder of the Bloomington Code School</u>

SOLUTION

The Bloomington Technology Partnership, comprised of the city of Bloomington, the Bloomington Economic Development Corporation, Indiana University's Innovate Indiana, and Indiana University's Office of Engagement, rallied local tech companies, public investment firms, and coding talent to come together – for free – in The Bloomington Code School.

Twelve weeks of courses on front-end web development, website design, PHP, JavaScript, and Rails development are guided by local tech experts, who act not just as teachers "but also to connect [students] to mentors outside the code school program," instructor Brandon Pfeiffer told Indiana Daily Student News. The Community Foundation of Bloomington and Monroe County provide a grant; the Monroe County Public Library provides free access to the online learning platforms; CFC Properties donates workspace; and Smithville Communications provides complimentary high-speed broadband access – all to create this community coding commons.

RESULTS

- The Bloomington Code School has had 200 students in just its first two years, with many graduates quickly finding local employment, according to the Bloomington Technology Partnership.

- According to the 2015 Hire Up Indy "Investment Strategies for Developing Tech Talent" report, the Bloomington Code School is setting the bar: "[They] have successfully prepared talent for the growing need for software developers in their respective communities through online learning programs that provide low-cost, flexible and self-paced training courses."

RESOURCES

- Bloomington Code School: bloomingtontech.com/bloomington-code-school

Freifunk:
Activists Who Provide Internet for All

♀ Münster, Germany

By Adrien Labaeye, with content provided by the Freifunk Münster group

PROBLEM

Internet access has become an essential part of life. However, many still cannot afford it. There are also growing concerns that internet connections could be unilaterally cut by Internet Service Providers at the request of public agencies. How do we ensure everyone has internet access?

SOLUTION

As early as 2002, the German activists of Freifunk, a noncommercial grassroots group, decided to self-organize to provide a free and autonomous internet infrastructure for all. In 2014, Münster free-internet activists from the local hacker space Warpzone decided to deploy a mesh network for their building complex. They visited a neighboring Freifunk community in Bielefeld that provided them with a crash course into the technology involved, which was mainly provided by the national Freifunk network.

The idea is that any WiFi router can be turned into an access point that communicates directly with other routers, passing along information between them, and thus forming a "mesh" of router-to-router connections. This way, people can send data from any point

"In 2015 we made contact with another community in our vicinity: Freifunk Warendorf. Instead of arguing about 'borders,' we decided to pool resources (servers, firmware, time of skilled people.)"

Anonymous Freifunk Münster activist

in the mesh without even connecting to the internet. The infrastructure is owned and maintained by the activists, who formed an association to handle legal and financial practicalities.

In 2015, Freifunk Münster joined with nearby Freifunk Warendorf to pool resources, including skilled people and IT infrastructure, and then made them available to the whole Münsterland region.

RESULTS

- In June 2015, the parliament of North Rhine-Westphalia (Landtag NRW) decided to support the local Freifunk initiatives by granting permission to use the roofs of buildings that belong to the state.

- In 2016, the Freifunk initiative was awarded 8,000 euros to build a wireless backbone over the city, bringing Freifunk to places with no internet connection and connecting the scattered little mesh clouds.

- Thanks to the growth of communities in western Münsterland, the mesh reached 2,000 access points on April 20, 2016, making it the largest mesh network in Germany.

RESOURCES

- Freifunk network: freifunk.net/en

- Freifunk community forum (German): forum.freifunk.net

Connecting.nyc:
Managing a Top-level Domain (.nyc) as a Commons

New York, New York, U.S.

By Adrien Labaeye

PROBLEM

The internet was initially built as a peer-to-peer network, but commercial interests
changed it into a highly market-driven system over time. Domains are one reason for
this change. Top-level domains such as .com and .net became resources that were
used to make a profit. In the past couple of years, this phenomenon has extended to
other domains like .nyc and .paris. Are there ways to secure these digital resources
so that they serve local communities?

SOLUTION

Back in 2000, Thomas Lowenhaupt, founding director of Connecting.nyc, imagined
that a ".nyc" domain could be used to support local online communications across New
York City's neighborhoods. The challenge was to ensure the attribution of the .nyc URLs
would be done to benefit residents of New York City and not be taken by commercial-
ly-driven interests.

On April 19, 2001, Lowenhaupt convinced the Queens Community Board to pass an
Internet Empowerment Resolution. The resolution called for the acquisition of the

> "Don't expect government to recognize and adopt something new just because it might be useful. The bureaucracy is severely restricted in doing innovative things. Organize and make them do the right thing."
>
> <u>Thomas Lowenhaupt, founding director of Connecting.nyc</u>

.nyc Top Level Domain, or TLD, and for its development as a public-interest resource to serve the residents and organizations of New York City.

Receiving no further institutional support, Lowenhaupt then started Connecting.nyc Inc. as a not-for-profit to advance the application and acquisition of the .nyc domain. Eventually, in 2008, a resolution was passed by the New York City Council to support the city's application for the .nyc domain.

In 2014, the Internet Corporation for Assigned Names and Numbers (the global institution governing the attribution of TLDs) delegated .nyc to Neustar, which manages the requests for attributions on behalf of the city administration, under a public-private partnership. Following connecting.nyc's recommendation, only New York City-based individuals and organizations can register a .nyc domain name and many second-level domain names have been set aside – for example, harlem.nyc. In 2016, the city administration initiated a program to license operators of 385 neighborhood domain names.

RESULTS

- 385 neighborhood names have been set aside to be licensed to public-interest organizations. 400 other names (beyond neighborhoods) have been reserved for public use.

- The Queens Community Board's Internet Empowerment Resolution was the first instance of a local government calling for the development of a TLD as a public-interest resource. Since then, cities have increasingly begun to look upon TLDs as a new urban space that provides opportunities and requires governance.

RESOURCES

- Connecting.nyc: www.connectingnyc.org/neighborhoods-home

Human Ecosystem Project:
Social Media Data Used to Analyze City Infrastructure and Citizen Well-being

♀ Bologna, Italy

—

By Adrien Labaeye

Social media networks and state intelligence agencies harvest massive amounts of data on their users. Private services primarily use the data to show targeted advertisements to their users, while government surveillance programs allegedly use the information for national security purposes. In both cases, the use of the data is neither transparent, nor is it used to directly help the people whose information is being collected.

Human Ecosystem Relazioni is a project funded by the city of Bologna to harness public information available from social media to understand what their citizens care about and how they are feeling at a given time and place in the city. The Human Ecosystems platform, on which this project relies, turns data from privately-owned social media platforms into open data that can be used by city officials, researchers, and the community at large. It is a way to identify trends and patterns that can lead to observations about the functioning of city infrastructure, and which can in turn lead to possible paths toward their improvement. The data can also be analyzed to produce interactive exhibits featuring a series of visualizations that demonstrate certain types of behavior and opinions among the citizens of Bologna. The Human Ecosystems platform has also been adopted in São Paulo, Brazil, and New Haven, U.S.

RESOURCES
• Human Ecosystems Relazioni (Italian): www.he-r.it

Smart Citizen Toolkit:
Monitoring City Air Quality with Crowdsourced Data

♀ Barcelona, Spain

By Adrien Labaeye

Air pollution is a critical public health issue that many cities are struggling to address. Aside from political disputes that can hinder regulatory solutions, there is also a broader obstacle to solving this challenge: the lack of accurate, publicly-accessible data that reflects the extent of the pollution on a real-time basis. This is why FabLab Barcelona, through a collaboration between technologists and citizen scientists, created the Smart Citizen Toolkit. It is a compact device that contains a data processor and a series of sensors that people use to monitor environmental conditions where they live.

Using the kit and the accompanying online platform, users can monitor such things as temperature, humidity, and carbon monoxide and nitrogen dioxide levels. The information is automatically uploaded to an independent platform that gathers the data from hundreds of distributed sensors. Since the published data can easily be made publicly accessible, universities, city governments, and anyone with the know-how can use the data for research on the local environment. The software and hardware for the toolkit are also all open-source. In addition to Barcelona, Amsterdam and Manchester have used it to measure air quality in their regions.

RESOURCES
• Smart Citizen: smartcitizen.me

PetaJakarta:

Disaster Response Management Through Crowdsourced Civic Data

♀ Jakarta, Indonesia

By Ryan T. Conway

Jakarta has long faced a host of challenges. It is one of the most densely populated cities in the world, and every year the area is battered by a monsoon. Since 40 percent of the city is at or below sea level, it regularly floods – a problem that will be exacerbated by the global sea-level rise induced by climate change. Jakarta also has one of the highest concentrations of active Twitter users in the world and a high proportion of cellphone use overall. That's why a public-private partnership between Twitter, Jakarta Emergency Management Agency, the University of Wollongong in Australia, and others developed CogniCity, an open-source intelligence framework that manages spatial data received from mobile messaging apps.

The first platform built on CogniCity was PetaJakarta, a Twitter-based crowdsourcing map for flood data. It relies on Twitter to organize and display real-time information about flooding to Jakarta residents. PetaJakarta allows users to geotag Tweets to indicate flooded areas, which are verified and added to a map of government flood alerts that anyone can use to navigate hazardous, urban terrain. The platform has been so successful that it has received international praise from organizations such as the International Federation of Red Cross and Red Crescent Societies.

RESOURCES

• PetaJakarta: petajakarta.org/banjir/en/index.html

ShareHub Connects Residents to Seoul's Local Sharing Economy

♀ Seoul, South Korea

By Shareable (adapted from this post: www.shareable.net/blog/sharehub-at-the-heart-of-seouls-sharing-movement)

Most residents of Seoul don't know about all the resources available through locally-owned sharing services and local government. The potential to reduce waste, connect people, and help residents save money by sharing goes mostly unrealized. That's why the heart of "Sharing City, Seoul" (see Chapter 4), is ShareHub, an online platform that connects users to sharing services, publishes sharing-related news, and is the online information hub for the city's Sharing City, Seoul project. After nearly five years in existence, ShareHub, which is operated by the nonprofit C.O.D.E. (formerly Creative Commons Korea), has served several million visitors and has played a key role in promoting sharing policies, projects, and culture in Seoul.

RESOURCES
• ShareHub: english.sharehub.kr

How to Stimulate $1 Billion in Economic Activity by Offering the Fastest, Cheapest Internet in the Western Hemisphere

♀ Chattanooga, Tennessee, U.S.

—

By Nikolas Kichler

Chattanooga, Tennessee, took a great leap in 2002 when its City Council passed Resolution No. 23446, authorizing their Electric Power Board (EPB) to provide internet services. It leaped again in 2007 when the City Council passed Resolution No. 25265, authorizing EPB to launch fiber-to-the-home gigabit-speed services by 2010 and 10-gigabit-speed services by 2016.

But before earning the "Gig City" moniker, Chattanooga was struggling to update its energy grid. Nevertheless, as an October 2016 Motherboard story reported, Chattanooga funded its smart grid through $169 million in municipal bonds and a $111 million U.S. Department of Energy stimulus grant, and launched broadband internet service in 2010.

According to the EPB's site, the network serves 75,000 businesses and households with what Mayor Andy Berke has claimed is the fastest, cheapest, and most pervasive broadband service in the Western Hemisphere. To reach even more residents, it rolled out its half-price $26.55 a month NetBridge service in 2015 to any household with a child eligible for the National School Lunch Program. According to a May 2016 CNN story, NetBridge attracted 1,700 eligible low-income families within its first year.

In 2015, an independent study, "The Realized Value of Fiber Infrastructure in Hamilton County, Tennessee," showed that Chattanooga's network created up to 5,200 new jobs and up to $1.3 billion in economic activity. Chattanooga has won awards and top tier media attention for its broadband service and the economic transformation it has catalyzed.

Chattanooga's example shows that by owning the infrastructure, city government can decide how to address such issues as the digital divide and net neutrality instead of relying on distant federal agencies. It can also take its economic destiny into its own hands rather than rely on commercial firms to provide the infrastructure needed for a 21st century economy.

VIEW THE FULL POLICIES

- Resolution No. 23446: ilsr.org/rule/2515-2

- Resolution No. 25265: www.chattanooga.gov/city-council-files/
  OrdinancesAndResolutions/Resolutions/Resolutions%202007/25265%20Auth%20
  EPB%20To%20Provice%20Add'l%20Services.doc

RESOURCES

- Economic-impact report on the value of fiber infrastructure in Hamilton County,
  Tennessee: ftpcontent2.worldnow.com/wrcb/pdf/091515EPBFiberStudy.pdf

- News story on U.S. government control over broadband service:
  www.onthecommons.org/magazine/who-gets-decide-what-city-can-do-
  broadband-internet

LiMux:
How to Save 11 Million Euros by Switching to Open-source Software

♀ Munich, Germany

By Adrien Labaeye

In 2003, Microsoft stopped supporting the Windows NT4 desktop operating system. As a result, Munich's city government had to migrate over 15,000 personal computers (PCs) to a new operating system. This made the disadvantages of dependence on big proprietary software providers obvious to local policy makers.

In 2004, the City Council decided to migrate its PCs to Linux, a free and open-source operating system, to achieve more independence and stimulate the local economy by using local developers for the migration. The choice for Linux was made despite the fact that Microsoft's CEO personally offered Munich a 90 percent discount on new software. The project, called LiMux, took seven years to complete and saved Munich over 11 million euros ($12.3 million). Other advantages include more flexibility in software management, better security, and a lower number of support calls.

However, not everybody is happy with the switch. A February 2017 ZDNet story reported on a proposal being drawn up by the city council to switch back to Windows, which has strong support on the council despite the fact that a large majority of recently surveyed LiMux users are satisfied.

RESOURCES

- News story on how the city managed the transition: opensource.com/government/14/5/how-munich-switched-15000-pcs-windows-linux

- News story on a proposal to switch back to Windows: www.zdnet.com/article/linuxs-munich-crisis-crunch-vote-locks-city-on-course-for-windows-return

Office of New Urban Mechanics Engages Residents in City Making

📍 Boston, Massachusetts, U.S.

—

By Shareable

In 2010, Boston's Mayor Menino formed the Mayor's Office of New Urban Mechanics (MONUM). MONUM is the city's civic innovation group. The purpose of MONUM is to engage residents, employees, communities, and institutions in the process of improving the quality of city services using technology. Through the group's current focal areas of economy, education, engagement, and streetscape, MONUM tests and scales new civic technologies. Innovations include open reporting through Citizens Connect, automated road quality reporting through Street Bump, and school-finding portal DiscoverBPS to name a few. Alongside MONUM, The Boston Urban Mechanics Program (BUMP) gives interns a chance to learn the challenges of improving city services first hand. These programs inspired many cities, including San Francisco and Philadelphia, to start similar programs.

RESOURCES

- Boston's Mayor's Office of New Urban Mechanics:
  www.cityofboston.gov/newurbanmechanics

City Open-data Policy

⦿ Montevideo, Uruguay

—

By Adrien Labaeye

In 2010, the city of Montevideo passed a resolution to make all data processed by the city administration (and not subject to privacy concerns) public. Since the resolution was enacted, an open-data portal was launched and over 50 datasets are now freely available. To bypass the burden of building its own new portal, Montevideo uses the national open-data portal that has been built upon the open-source software CKAN developed by the Open Knowledge Foundation, a global standard which is easily replicable. This policy spurred the development of many new apps that are using the data in both traditional and original ways. Public transport timetables, a map facilitating bicycle commuting, an app showing what taxes are spent on, and tools for finding recycling bins are joined by other, more unexpected uses, like a map showing that only 10 percent of streets are named after women. This is surely just the beginning; as additional data becomes available, new innovative applications will be sure to follow.

RESOURCES
- Montevideo's open data portal (Spanish):
  www.montevideo.gub.uy/institucional/montevideo-abierto/datos-abiertos

Cities Use Creative Commons Licenses to Give the Public Permission to Use All Kinds of City Data

♀ Worldwide

—

By Neal Gorenflo

Creative Commons (CC) is a U.S. nonprofit that enables owners of any kind of data – from blog posts to design files to data sets to photographs – to make their data available for use without prior permission through a set of licenses that make clear to prospective users who and how the data can be used. It augments copyright law and makes a freer flow of information in society possible while giving content owners the level of control over their intellectual property they desire. Cities around the world are using Creative Commons' free, easy-to-use licenses in a number of ways. The city of Buenos Aires uses a CC BY 2.5 license for their entire website. Vienna, Austria, uses a CC BY license for their Open Government Data Portal. Wellington City Council, in New Zealand, offers datasets of aerial imagery, contours, building footprints, flood hazards, wind zones, and more under a CC BY license. Washington, D.C., has made the DC code available under a CC0 Public Domain Dedication.

RESOURCES

• About Creative Commons licenses: creativecommons.org/licenses

• A list of how governments are using Creative Commons licenses: wiki.creativecommons.org/wiki/Government_use_of_Creative_Commons

Deputy Mayor for Free Software and Open Data

9 Grenoble, France

—

By Adrien Labaeye

When a coalition comprised of the green party and multiple civic movements worked together to win the municipal election in Grenoble in 2014, Eric Piolle – a former and rebellious executive at Hewlett-Packard – became the new mayor. Soon after, he appointed a deputy mayor for Open Data and Free Software, committing to move the city toward free and open-source software and support its deployment. The goals were to facilitate knowledge sharing, emancipation of individuals and institutions, and to save money. In 2015, the city administration became a member of the French association for free software (April), confirming its commitment.

In February 2016, the effects of the policy started to become visible with the release of a software under an open-source license (GPLv3) by the city administration. The product, called AGAPE, is an interface for schools to manage online access to learning material. By making it available as free software, the city of Grenoble hopes that other cities will be able to use it, saving on an investment made unnecessary, making the best use of public money.

RESOURCES

- Deputy mayor for Open Data and Free Software (official profile, French): www.grenoble.fr/122-laurence-comparat.htm

- French association for free software (April): www.april.org/en

- City press release (French): www.grenoble.fr/uploads/Externe/fd/77_364_La-Ville-de-Grenoble-devoile-AGAPE-ECOLE.pdf

Increasing Engagement and Addressing the Digital Divide

9 Wellington, New Zealand

By Ryan T. Conway

The Wellington City Council began developing municipal technology policies in 1995, when their Info City project first emerged. This led to a broadband network in the business district, free web hosting for community groups, and improved access to computers for addressing the digital divide, as published by Wellington's School of Information Management and the 20/20 Trust.

In 2006, they advanced further with their Information and Communications Technology Policy. This unique policy focuses on "e-Community" and "e-Democracy." The former aims to "build capability and capacity in the community so that all can participate in an economy and society that has an increasing reliance on ICT," while the latter's provisions are "to encourage an increased and enhanced level of engagement in the Council's decision-making processes and to provide efficient access to Council services."

VIEW THE FULL POLICY

- wellington.govt.nz/~/media/your-council/plans-policies-and-bylaws/plans-and-policies/a-to-z/ict/files/ictpolicy.pdf?la=en

"

WE ARE CAUGHT IN AN INESCAPABLE NETWORK OF MUTUALITY, TIED IN A SINGLE GARMENT OF DESTINY.

– DR. MARTIN LUTHER KING JR.

FINANCE

Today we constantly hear grievances about there not being enough money for this or that beneficial cause. But at the same time, many people have huge privately managed assets that finance all kinds of ventures through retirement investments – some of which they would probably not wish to support. We often keep these funds out of fear for our long-term security.

What would happen if people mobilized these vast assets in shared projects to create a better and more stable future in their own communities? By pooling citizens' wealth for community purposes rather than simply for the highest returns, money and credit can be made much more abundant to ordinary people. Finance enables communities to flourish, to pool their common wealth, to share and thereby reduce risk, and to achieve objectives that individuals cannot achieve alone.

The tools to implement this imagined future already exist. Finance of this kind funds projects that do not offer quick returns on investment, but are immensely important for our continued well-being and the stability of natural ecosystems. Needs-oriented finance takes public needs seriously, which also means that benefits and risks are shared equitably. This is only possible if all people involved share in the ownership, responsibility, and decision-making.

The case studies in this chapter present solutions to realize this vision of shared finance in cities. The selected cases are meant to cover the main actors at the level of the city – that is, citizens, businesses, financial institutions, and the local government. Furthermore, we have tried to cover many aspects of finance – including the creation of money, savings and investments, and mutual security.

So let us start with what citizens can do.

First, citizens can create means of exchange that take on some of the functions of money, and determine the rules governing their circulation. Generally, central and private banks enjoy the privilege of creating money, which is one of the factors leading to the accumulation of wealth in the hands of a few. The attempts so far to create alternative systems of exchange, like community currencies, are generally small or specialized, but they can have significant benefits for the participants and demonstrate how we might redesign the institution of money on a large scale.

Second, citizens can use their money to invest in enterprises they wish to support, providing mutual benefits to the entire community. The investment fund for local sustainable food production in Freiburg, Germany, and civic crowdfunding by Spacehive in the U.K. both focus on investment. The first example uses money as savings, while the other seeks only nonfinancial returns on investments.

Third, citizens can pool their money as well as their time, skills, ideas, and knowledge in order to provide mutual financial security. Sickness and old age are two of the main financial risk factors we all face. The Fureai Kippu time banks in Japan address these issues. It is a case where a successful social welfare system has been established to ensure financial security in case of illness and old age.

What can businesses do? They can provide mutual credit as a means of exchange, and facilitate mutually beneficial trading relationships, both of which tend to increase stability in the face of economic downturns. The WIR Bank of Switzerland, essentially a network of small and medium enterprises, has successfully performed all these business-to-business functions ever since the depression years of the 1930s.

Specialized financial institutions with a well-defined mission for the public or the common good also have an important role to play. They can be public, cooperative, or socially driven institutions.

Cooperative financial institutions are owned by the people or institutions that rely on their services, which ensures accountability to the people they serve. As a particularly successful example, we have featured the Self-Help Credit Union of North Carolina, in the United States. It is part of a broader category of community development financial institutions (CDFIs) in the United States, which have as their mission to promote economic opportunity among minority and other disadvantaged communities. Customer-owned and cooperative banks play an important role in many other countries as well, and generally provide financial services at reasonable cost, while investing primarily in the local economy.

Socially driven financial institutions devoted to the common good can also follow a variety of other institutional models, belonging to foundations, trusts, or other institutions. A number of such banks have come together to form the Global Alliance for Banking on Values. We have featured a bank that does not belong to this alliance, but is remarkable for the local economic development work it is promoting in Brazil and the local currency it has launched: Banco Palmas. It follows a hybrid ownership model, involving the local communities and the non-profit organization Instituto Palmas.

How can local governments support shared finance? They can establish policy goals to support those building blocks of shared finance that already exist in a place and help them grow, to help establish new tools, and to help create mutually supportive connections. A local government can support its own citizens' efforts in alternative finance. Cities can even set up or support their own financial institutions, as the U.S. state of North Dakota has done. Although this is strictly speaking a state – and not a city – policy, it should be noted that North Dakota has a population of only around 700,000 people, which is easily exceeded by the population of many metropolitan areas. This means that many cities would be able to start banks that would have at least as much business and profit potential as the Bank of North Dakota.

The cases featured in this chapter are drawn from diverse places, and yet, they could surely have been much more diverse than they are. What is in a way even more unfortunate is that it would be difficult to find a single place where all these types of institutions flourish. Which city in the world will be the first to develop a complete network of institutions, policies and practices to finance the emergence of a truly sustainable economy that supports the aspirations of all its people? This would be a challenge worthy of a Sharing City!

Wolfgang Hoeschele

People visiting the site of a proposed linear park, the "Peckham Coal Line" in London, that successfully raised funds through the Spacehive crowdfunding site. Photographer: Louise Armstrong. Source: Unsplash. Usage rights: CC BY-NC-SA 4.0

Spacehive:
Enabling Crowdfunding for Civic Projects

♀ London, U.K.

By Wolfgang Hoeschele

PROBLEM

There are many urban spaces that have the potential to become lively community hubs but sit empty due to little or no funding. Through crowdfunding, it's possible to access a large number of people to raise money for important causes. How can we tap into this power of crowdfunding to raise money for civic projects?

SOLUTION

Spacehive is a crowdfunding platform for civic projects that bring various places in the U.K. to life. Like other crowdfunding sites, Spacehive facilitates the process of fundraising, complementing conventional methods (loans from banks or individuals, investment funds, grants from local government and foundations) that may be inaccessible or excessively onerous.

The projects are oriented to the needs of the people who initiate them, the people they hope to serve, and the people who fund them. For example, one successful project, the Peckham Coal Line, is now in the stage of doing a feasibility study. The idea is to create a linear park that is a pleasant route to walk or cycle in Peckham (a

London district). The people who helped fund the project expect to benefit by being able to use the park themselves. Spacehive is not available for soliciting loans or investments, meaning that funders do not expect a financial return.

Benefits accrue not only to the people directly involved, but potentially to everyone in the neighborhood of funded projects. Projects that change the place in some long-term way have to go through ordinary public approval processes to ensure that they are of public benefit.

The Spacehive platform itself receives 5 percent of the donated money in order to fund its own operations. This overhead charge makes this site possible. The original investment funds to develop the site came from social investment funds, primarily Big Society Capital and Si² Fund. Ultimately, benefits will also accrue to the investors in those funds.

The risk if a project fails is that funders get no benefit in return for the money they donated, and that project initiators fail to accomplish their goals. In order to minimize risk to funders, Spacehive works with Locality to provide a verification service which checks if the project idea is viable and can be delivered once the funding target has been met. The delivery manager for the project must agree to Spacehive's terms and conditions which ensure the money raised will solely be spent on delivering the project as described.

RESULTS
- As of June 2017, Spacehive had raised £6.7 million ($8.5 million) for 306 projects since its inception in 2012.

- The average project raised £21,895 ($27,898), 52 percent of projects reach their funding goal, and 99% were successfully delivered.

- Numerous cities have partnered with Spacehive (see an example of this from London in "Mayor-supported Civic Crowdfunding Program").

RESOURCES
- Peckham Coal Line: www.spacehive.com/peckhamcoalline

- Report on alternative finance trends in Europe: publications.europa.eu/en/publication-detail/-/publication/3190dbeb-316e-11e7-9412-01aa75ed71a1

Banco Palmas:
Building a Solidarity Socio-economy

◊ Conjunto Palmeira, Brazil

By Leila Collins

PROBLEM

The Conjunto Palmeira, created by local fishermen who were pushed inland when the coast of Brazil was developed and became prime real estate in the 1970s, became a poor suburban community of 32,000 people close to Fortaleza, a city of 2.5 million. Most of the residents were unable to make a basic income as their livelihood had been dependent on the sea, which had become inaccessible. Not only were the local authorities unable to provide welfare, they also did not provide basic infrastructure. As a result, there were no competitive businesses in Conjunto Palmeira, so most goods circulating in the community were sourced from Fortaleza. What could be done to uplift this community?

SOLUTION

In 1989, with a donation from a French organization, members of the local community launched Banco Palmas, a community development bank designed to address local unemployment and stimulate local spending. Community organizers Joaquim Melo and Francisco Bezerra got the bank off the ground by building strong con-

"To date, hundreds of local businesses have signed up to accept Palmas, while the currency has helped strengthen or create thousands of local livelihoods."

Christian Hiss, Regionalwert AG (translated from German)

nections with existing local banks. In 2003, Banco Palmas launched a local currency to complement the Brazilian real called "palmas." The currency was designed to foster local pride, designed by local artists complete with security features. Still running today, Banco Palmas aims to keep the money spent in the neighborhood circulating in the neighborhood to ensure local development.

Banco Palmas offers a range of microcredit for individuals who would otherwise not qualify for traditional loans for small businesses, personal consumption in the community (with palmas), and for housing renovations. In 2010, Banco Palmas also began offering a small microinsurance option.

The bank is managed entirely by local people. Palmas Institute, a nonprofit, administers the circulation of Banco Palmas with six full-time staff. It is funded by grants in addition to account fees and transaction fees.

RESULTS

- Banco Palmas has proven that it is possible to stimulate local economic development regardless of the level of poverty of the community. The bank has supported the local identity and economy while creating 1,800 jobs (including currency and credit services). By 2011, 270 businesses were involved with 46,000 palmas ($22,243) in circulation.

- Palmas are now the exclusive source of currency for some people. Both the Brazilian government and the central bank of Brazil have championed Banco Palmas. Sixty-six communities around the world have used Banco Palmas as a model for their local banks.

- As Banco Palmas revitalized the Conjunto Palmeira economy, crime rates dropped and the general quality of life improved.

RESOURCES

- Banco Palmas (Portuguese): www.institutobancopalmas.org

Vegetable market in Münsterplatz, Freiburg im Breisgau, Baden-Württemberg, Germany. Photographer: Daderot. Usage rights: CC0 1.0

Regionalwert AG:
Citizen Investment in a Sustainable Local Food System

⚲ Freiburg, Germany

By Wolfgang Hoeschele

PROBLEM

The development of sustainable local food production requires long-term investments. These investments often yield relatively low rates of return. Distribution poses additional challenges because conventional buyers demand large quantities, and small-scale distribution methods such as community-supported agriculture may require a lot of time and effort. Artisanal food processors face similar issues. How do we address these problems in producing food locally?

SOLUTION

A corporation called "Regionalwert AG" (Regional Value Inc., or RWAG) was formed in Freiburg, Germany, to funnel the investments of urban residents to buy shares in sustainable agricultural and food businesses in the region. This way, concerned urban consumers, farmers, food processors, and retailers share the responsibility and the benefits of investing in sustainable food production within the region.

This corporation has some special features. It uses social and ecological selection criteria as to which businesses it will support. While the businesses remain independent and

"The greatest challenge is to raise the awareness of everyone involved that the return on investment consists of more than money."

Source: LocalFutures.org

FINANCE | Case Study

make their own entrepreneurial decisions, the approval of RWAG as an investor/ shareholder of the partner business is required for certain business transactions.

RWAG facilitates regular meetings among business managers to promote the establishment of relationships that enable equitable sharing of the economic benefits and risks. Annual reports include not only the financial results, but also the ecological and social benefits obtained. Investors do not simply obtain a financial return, but are also called on to contribute their knowledge to the vitality of the businesses in which they have invested. Shareholders have voting rights proportional to the shares they own, but no person may have more than 20 percent of the voting rights. Shares are issued to a named person, who can sell the shares to another named person only with the permission of the board. This rule ensures that most shareholders keep their shares for a long-term and can also prevent concentration of ownership among a few persons.

RESULTS

- From its founding in 2006 until 2014, about 500 shareholders invested over 2 million euros, helping a number of businesses get established or expand. As of May 2016, the businesses in the network include six farms (organic gardening, vegetable production, dairy, pork production, winery, and fruit liquors), a catering business, two food processors (salad dressings, dried fruits), a wholesaler, five retailers (including a CSA-service for the farms in the network), a business consultant, an accounting firm, and a nonprofit research service.

- An organic, vegetarian, regionally-based restaurant is about to be opened.

- Numerous business relationships link these companies, that are all committed to organic and regional food production.

- The term "Regionalwert" has been trademarked, two offshoots have been founded in Hamburg and Cologne, and a third is being started in Munich. Meanwhile, in Frankfurt, a "Bürger AG" has been started with a similar but not identical business model.

RESOURCES

- Case study on community-connected farming:
  www.forum-synergies.eu/docs/a012_rwag.pdf

Nippon Active Life Club:
Time Banking for Affordable Elderly Care

Multiple Locations, Japan

By Ryan T. Conway

In a country like Japan, where people over the age of 65 make up more than a quarter of the population, a pressing question is how the elderly can be provided with quality care without it becoming a major strain on the rest of the tax-paying population. Since the 1970s, time banking approaches have been developed there to address this problem. In Japanese, these practices are collectively called "fureai kippu." People who help the elderly earn time credits, which they can redeem themselves when they grow old, or gift to older family members living in other cities. Such credits can be supplemented with cash payments. Those who commit their time are generally not professional caregivers. Therefore, most of the care work includes basic services such as cleaning, yard work, and general companionship. Some of the time banks are run by local governments or quasi-governmental organizations. The largest number of them belong to a nonprofit network called Nippon Active Life Club. The club operates a time bank supported by member dues, and members pay for care work in both time credits and cash. As of early 2016, it had nearly 18,000 members and 124 offices across the country.

RESOURCES
- Nipon Active Life Club: nalc.jp/English.htm

- Sawayaka Welfare Foundation (Japanese): www.sawayakazaidan.or.jp

Self-help Credit Union:
Nonprofit Financial Services for Underserved Communities

◊ Durham, North Carolina, U.S.

By Wolfgang Hoeschele

Community development initiatives, such as cooperatives and local food projects, require financial services that many conventional banks do not offer. At the same time, most major banks do not provide underserved communities with services to help secure their well-being. The Self-Help Credit Union is a Community Development Financial Institution with a mission to create opportunities for people who would otherwise not be able to obtain reasonable financing terms. Its main focus is on assisting marginalized people and locally-oriented enterprises. It is a network of two credit unions, a nonprofit loan fund, and policy advocacy organization. The credit unions offer a wide array of standard financial services to individuals and community development projects, such as checking and savings accounts and loans. Its advocacy arm is involved in promoting fair lending practices across the United States. Since 1980, when the Self-Help Credit Union began in Durham, North Carolina, it has gradually expanded its business by merging with similar credit unions across North Carolina, California, Florida, and Illinois. This larger network is called the Self-Help Federal Credit Union, which has 40 branches serving 130,000 people.

RESOURCES
• Self-Help Credit Union: www.self-help.org

• Self-Help Federal Credit Union: www.self-helpfcu.org

WIR Bank:

Cooperatively-managed Electronic Currency for Community Economic Development

◍ Multiple Locations, Switzerland

—

By Leila Collins

The Great Depression of 1929 was felt globally. In Switzerland, it triggered a mass currency shortage, leaving businesses unable to buy or sell their goods and services. In response to the crisis, a board of progressive thinkers formed the "Wirtschafts-ring-Genossenschaft" (German for "economic circle cooperative"), an independent system to supplement the national currency. When it was created in 1934, the founders' aim was to serve small and medium-sized enterprises (SMEs) by enabling them to extend lines of credit to each other. In 1998, it expanded its offering of financial services and renamed itself the WIR Bank. Since then, the cooperative bank has created the WIR Franc, an electronic currency system whose value remains equal to one Swiss Franc. The bank issues the WIR Franc by extending interest-free lines of credit, or loans, to its community members. The WIR Bank incentivizes business members to conduct business transactions with other members, thereby creating an affinity network between them. The WIR Bank has grown to more 60,000 members, including 45,000 SMEs from across Switzerland. In 2010, 1.63 billion Swiss francs ($1.66 billion) were traded among its members.

RESOURCES

- Wir Bank (German): www.wir.ch/ueber-wir/wer-und-was-ist-wir

- Community Currency Knowledge Gateway on WIR Bank:
  community-currency.info/en/currencies/wir-bank

" YOUR WORK IS TO DISCOVER YOUR WORK AND THEN, WITH ALL YOUR HEART, TO GIVE YOURSELF TO IT.

– BUDDHA

The Bank of North Dakota:
Reliable Financing for the Common Good

⬩ North Dakota, U.S.

By Leila Collins with support from Matt Stannard and Marc Armstrong
(Public Banking Institute)

Most banking and credit is controlled by private banks that prioritize profit over community needs. Unfortunately, this sometimes leads private banks to fund unethical projects, defraud customers, seek bailouts when risky investments fail, or simply offer unattractive fees and interest rates. Most private banks profits flow out of local communities instead of stimulating the local economy. And, as in the subprime crisis, their mistakes can lead to economy-stifling credit shortages and other negative impacts to cities and their residents.

However, most cities deposit their funds in, and get their financing from, private banks. This exposes cities to their disadvantages. Cities, however, can follow the example of the state of North Dakota and form a government owned and controlled public bank. The Bank of North Dakota (BND) is a public bank that holds all state funds and is chartered to make safe, low-interest loans against this reserve to fund local businesses and projects. In addition, all of BND's profits go into the state treasury to fund schools, social programs, and other needs of state residents.

In a case decided by the U.S. Supreme Court (Green versus Frazier, 253 U.S. 233) in 1919, the state government of North Dakota won the right to have its own bank. Since that decision, the BND has been guided by its charter to "serve the people of North Dakota." Following the charter, the BND has focused on low-risk, local lending done primarily through a network of independent community banks. It has only one location and does little retail banking, so complements rather than competes with banks.

In other ways, the BND is run like a typical for-profit bank. BND is staffed with professional bankers and lending decisions are made based on conventional criteria, though it is more likely to fund community-enhancing projects that typical banks.

BND has been profitable since at least 1971 (the furthest back records are available) and has grown to $4 billion in assets. The state's government and economy has benefited substantially from BND's long-lived and consistent success. BND has contributed hundreds of millions of dollars to the state treasury over its lifetime ($300 million between 1998 and 2008 alone). BND has helped North Dakota maintain a low unemployment rate, large state government budget surpluses, a robust network of community banks, and high credit availability even during economic crises.

BND is no anomaly. Public banks have a long history of success in other countries such as Costa Rica and Germany. Because of BND and other successful public banks' track record, a number of U.S. cities and states are pursuing or have pursued public banking legislation, including the city of Oakland in California and the state of Massachusetts. Much of this activity was sparked by the subprime crisis.

RESOURCES

- The Public Banking Institute: www.publicbankinginstitute.org

- Report on why governments should not use private banks: rooseveltinstitute.org/wp-content/uploads/2015/11/Bhatti_Dirty_Deals.pdf

- Feasibility study for a public bank in Massachusetts with a BND review: www.monetary.org/wp-content/uploads/2016/03/The-bank-of-north-dakota-a-model-for-mAss.pdf

The Brixton Pound (B£):
A Currency Designed to Benefit the Local Community

London, U.K.

By Leila Collins

The Brixton district in South London's Lambeth borough has been a bastion of progressive thought and culture for decades. After the financial crisis of 2008, local businesses were struggling and had trouble securing loans from banks. An area that had once thrived began to stumble.

The Brixton Pound (the B£) was launched in 2009 by Transition Town Brixton to support local businesses with a local currency that would "stick to Brixton." The founders of the B£ wanted to create a mutual support system tying residents to local businesses and encouraging business to source locally.

The local borough government, Lambeth Council, was supportive of the B£ from the beginning. It recognized the local currency as a way to develop the community, build local economic resilience, and draw positive attention to the area. According to B£ Communications Manager, Marta Owczarek, "The council's support has greatly helped the B£ start and develop – it would have been very difficult to do what we did without that support. In particular, it acted as a guarantee that the scheme was trustworthy, so local business owners and residents alike felt secure in exchanging their money into and accepting the brand-new local currency."

Within the first six months of the launch of the B£, Lambeth conducted research that estimated the media coverage of the currency generated by the B£ volunteers was worth half a million pounds to the area.

Since 2012, the B£ has "been a live part of the Co-operative Council, working alongside the policy team," according to Owczarek. As a result, the B£ has been able to play an active role in supporting the community while receiving council support. The B£ helped set up community spaces like the Impact Hub in the Town Hall. Lambeth helped the B£ create a mobile electronic payments system, and was also the first council to pay wages in local currency and accept a local currency for taxes. In 2014, the Lambeth Co-Operative Investment Fund gave the B£ funding to start a community lottery program, which was launched in 2015. The lottery increased the circulation of the B£, became an additional revenue source for the B£, and enabled the B£ to fund community projects.

The B£ has also helped Lambeth gain prominence globally and locally. In 2012, thanks to encouragement from the B£, the Council secured funding to join an international project to expand community currencies. On a local level, Lambeth won the Mayor's High Street Fund to install a local currency cash machine, possibly the first in the world.

RESOURCES

- Website for The Brixton Pound: brixtonpound.org

- Lambeth Council: www.lambeth.gov.uk

- Shareable's guide to starting a local currency:
  www.shareable.net/blog/how-to-start-a-community-currency

Community Benefits Agreements Extend the Benefits of New Real Estate Developments to the Wider Community

♀ Los Angeles, California, U.S.

By Wolfgang Hoeschele

New urban real estate developments often benefit investors and the affluent while providing few benefits for local residents of modest means. In fact, they often drive the poorest out of their own communities while providing few or no funds for urgent investments in public infrastructure.

To address these issues, an urban authority includes certain conditions into its contracts with real estate developers. The developers must make certain investments that contribute to the local community and adhere to labor and other practices designed to ensure that local working people benefit substantially from the policy. This makes funding available for public parks, affordable housing, schools, child care, or other needs, depending on a community's priorities.

This approach was pioneered by the Los Angeles Alliance for a New Economy (LAANE). It was used when a new sports stadium was built and the LAX airport was expanded. The latter agreement secured $500 million in job training and environmental benefits for affected residents and has helped create safer schools and neighborhoods for hundreds of thousands of local residents.

VIEW THE FULL POLICY

- LAANE website featuring several community benefits agreements: laane.org/policies

RESOURCES

- Park East Redevelopment Compact community benefit agreement in Milwaukee, Wisconsin:
  parkeastmke.com/wp-content/uploads/2014/02/Attachment-Q-PERC-FINAL.pdf

- Shareable's guide to negotiating a community benefit agreement:
  www.shareable.net/blog/how-to-negotiate-a-community-benefits-agreement-0

Mayor-supported Civic Crowdfunding Program

◊ London, U.K.

—

By Wolfgang Hoeschele

The London Mayor's Office has teamed up with the U.K.-based civic crowd-funding service Spacehive to support community-driven initiatives throughout the city.

Local groups placing projects on the platform can apply for a pledge from the Mayor of up to £20,000 ($25,960). The "Regeneration" office (which belongs to the Greater London Authority) uses several criteria to judge the projects. Their endorsement not only gives a direct financial boost, but also makes the projects more visible and credible for other potential donors, thus attracting more and bigger donations. The city government assists in other ways as well, such as setting up meetings with key stakeholders and helping project initiators to find good consultants to maximize impact and to support delivery. The goal is to innovate with a limited amount of money, empower people to participate in developing the city, and promote citizen power and new forms of engagement.

According to the city of London's website, 57 projects have been supported in the first three rounds; with £800,000 ($1.03 million) worth of pledges made by the Mayor, leveraging more than £900,000 ($1.16 million) of crowdfunding match from more than 6,000 backers. Campaigns backed by the Mayor had a 95 percent success rate, compared to a 47 percent average success rate for those that did not get such support.

Initial evaluation has revealed significant social impact. Local groups delivering projects have cited increased civic pride, skill development, new community bonds and improved knowledge of the planning and development process as consequences of the program.

RESOURCES

● Program website: www.london.gov.uk/what-we-do/regeneration/funding-opportunities/crowdfunding-programme

City-supported Time Banks

◊ Barcelona, Spain

By Wolfgang Hoeschele

Starting a new timebank requires a community that is ready to share their time and skills, but in order for it to be successful, there is also the need for a professional service and access to various facilities, including office, meeting, and event space. It can be difficult to organize and find these services and places based on donations and voluntary work contributions alone, so municipal aid can go a long way.

The city of Barcelona provides support to timebanks by providing educational and legal advice through its technical unit "Associació Salut i Família" (Health and Family Association). They offer municipal grants to entities or individuals that carry out activities or projects of public or social interest to the municipality, providing meeting spaces in neighborhood and civic centers, and offering advice and education to civic associations through its Torre Jussana center.

Partly as a result of this strong support from the city administration, Barcelona is regarded as one of the world's leading time-bank cities. Numerous time banks have emerged in the city, and offer training for those interested in starting time banks elsewhere in the world.

RESOURCES

- City of Barcelona's Time Bank website: w110.bcn.cat/portal/site/UsosDel Temps/menuitem.3bf0b3f28e0a377cf740f740a2ef8a0c/index6233.html?vgnextoid=9990cfab893a7310VgnVCM10000072fea8c0RCRD&vgnextchannel=9990cfab893a7310VgnVCM10000072fea8c0RCRD&lang=en_GB

Bank On San Francisco:
Supporting Community Financial Empowerment

San Francisco, California, U.S.

By Tom Llewellyn

Lacking access to a bank account greatly increases one's vulnerability to a variety of financial threats, including check cashing services, predatory "payday" lenders, theft, or simply losing cash. A 2008 study by the Brookings Institute found that, across the U.S., "moderate- and lower-income households pay over $8 billion in fees to non-bank check-cashing and short-term loan providers to meet their basic financial services needs."

In 2005, the city of San Francisco conducted a study and determined there were 50,000 households possessing neither a checking nor savings account. The study also found that people of color were disproportionately affected, with approximately 50 percent of African-American and Latino adults being "unbanked." To address this issue, a coalition of city officials, local and national government agencies, banks and credit unions, and community organizations came together to create the first Bank On program in the U.S.

According to the San Francisco Office of Financial Empowerment, its primary objectives were to:

- Change policies: Create more opportunities for lower-income clients to enter the financial mainstream.

- Modify accounts: Create products without high fees or minimum balances.

- Raise awareness: Help unbanked people learn about the benefits of keeping their money in checking and savings accounts.

- Provide financial education: Help San Franciscans learn more about how to use, manage, and save money.

As reported on their website, the initiative has been a big success, with 10,000 new checking accounts being opened each year since the program began in 2006.

RESOURCES

- Bank On San Francisco: bankonsanfrancisco.com

- San Francisco Office of Financial Empowerment:
  sfgov.org/ofe/ofe-bank-san-francisco

"

WITHOUT COMMUNITY, THERE IS NO LIBERATION.

– AUDRE LORDE

GOVERNANCE

Cities have been caught in the middle of a clash: they
are stuck competing for business investments while,
simultaneously, seeking to meet the needs of their
inhabitants through access to public goods and social
services. For this reason, there is no surprise in seeing
two opposite trends growing globally: on the one
hand, the commodification of cities – where public
spaces are sold to private buyers at the expense of
citizens fenced out by these transactions; on the other
hand, and likely in reaction to this privatization, there
is a growing trend where cities are turning into ecosystems for collaboration, cooperation, and sharing.

Pressure is especially mounting from social movements that are asserting claims to urban governance by invoking a "Right to the City" – a slogan proposed by Henri Lefebvre in his 1968 book, "Le Droit à la ville." This can be generally characterized as the collective right of urban inhabitants to have control in the decision making processes concerning public spaces, city resources, and other factors that shape their lives. The "Movimento dos Trabalhadores Sem Teto" in Brazil, Reclaim the Streets in the U.K., and the Gezi Park protests in Turkey are all examples of this. Yet, the effectiveness of these movements has been limited, due to a lack of conceptual or legal frameworks that could connect their movements and advance their claims to a Right to the City.

In "The City as a Commons," Sheila Foster and Christian Iaione propose an urban commons framework that provides new ways of seeing and creating the city, itself, as a commons. It is also a valuable way of thinking about how people can exercise their Right to the City. They explain how if collective action of a community is what creates common wealth from a shared resource, then the activities themselves are what creates wealth from the city. This can be a way to grant each person a right to that wealth, and a right to any decision making processes regarding the distribution of that wealth. This is distinct from commoning – a type of governance that is based on self-organized sharing arrangements – which is characterized by the sharing of authority, the sharing of power, and the sharing of control, relying wholly upon collective action and collective accountability.

The case studies and model policies in this chapter exemplify such systems of urban collaborative governance. Some cities in particular are leading this process: Bologna and Gdańsk have both reinvented themselves through a process of citizen participation. In Nairobi, Kenya, residents of one of the world's most infamous slums co-design urban commons with the help of accessible technologies, while disaster-stricken and marginalized communities of New Orleans in Louisiana self-organize trainings and gather resources that empower them to have an impact on the urban planning process.

Likewise, city-level model policies are detailed for the purpose of outlining steps that can be taken and replicated almost anywhere. Such is the case of Porto Alegre in Brazil, known for its robust participatory-budgeting project. We also see Los Angeles, California, keep its districts from feeling neglected by legally empowering a vast system of neighborhood councils. Meanwhile, South Korea's capital Seoul pools tax revenues to give each of its districts more equal services, and Dortmund in Germany makes a polycentric policy for mitigating and adapting to climate change.

These examples demonstrate why urban commons are so important for a Sharing City. When there are more urban commons, more residents can directly experience the effectiveness and empowerment of sharing practices. They cultivate the skills needed to create a Sharing City by commoning over smaller urban resources, like parks, and becoming more familiar with working together and sharpening their capacities to govern the whole city as a commons. These communities show how – with the right mix of commoning – all cities could become Sharing Cities.

Ryan T. Conway and Marco Quaglia

The Care and Regeneration of the Urban Commons

⚲ Bologna, Italy

By LabGov

PROBLEM

There is a crucial legal gap in the management of cities – it is often illegal for citizens to improve or maintain public spaces, parks, abandoned buildings, and other urban commons that directly impact their lives. Regulation using institutional technology and public collaboration is necessary to mitigate this issue.

SOLUTION

In 2014, the city of Bologna adopted the Regulation on Collaboration Between Citizens and the City for the Care and Regeneration of Urban Commons and launched "the city as a commons" project. The regulation and project represent a new and important legal and administrative framework for citizens to directly care for urban commons in Bologna and beyond.

Behind the scenes, the Fondazione del Monte di Bologna and Ravenna, LabGov, and innovators within the city paved the way with two years of field experiments applying co-governance methods to the management of urban commons. The bulk of the learning was accomplished through three "urban experimentation labs" with citizens and essential urban resources such as green spaces and abandoned buildings. The output of the research was the world's first regulation and administrative process outlining how cities and the citizens can collaborate to co-manage urban commons.

A key tool supporting the regulation are "collaboration pacts." A collaboration pact defines the specific commons in question and the rules for collaboration between stakeholders, including the city government. Collaboration pacts can be designed and signed by a single individual, informal groups, communities, and nonprofit organizations. They regulate both single, short-term interventions and long-term care of the urban commons. The regulation also fosters the creation of hyperlocal institutions for urban co-governance like community cooperatives, neighborhood foundations, and block consortia. Importantly, the regulation provides for the transfer of technical and monetary support from the city government to citizens. It also promotes citizen action in five categories: social innovation and collaborative services, urban creativity, digital innovation, collaborative communication, and collaborative tools and practices that foster urban commoning.

RESULTS

- More than 180 collaboration pacts have been signed in Bologna since the approval of the regulation. The regulation, collaboration pacts, and associated administrative processes have become an "administrative good practice" on a global basis. The regulation has also triggered the design of a broad urban co-governance program. Building on the success of the regulation, Bologna launched "Collaborare è Bologna" (CO-Bologna), an innovative public policy with two main purposes:

    - Coordinating several projects and policies on the regeneration of the urban commons through social innovation and collaborative economy. Key achievements include the Pilastro and Incredibol projects.

    - Prototyping a process and institutional infrastructure to keep experimenting with the urban commons movement. To be sure, CO-Bologna is structured as an open collaboration that seeks to involve whoever is willing to practice civic imagination in the city.

- The long-term goal of the project is to lay the foundation for the transformation of Bologna into a co-city with a robust collaborative ecosystem. Building on the care and regeneration of the city, efforts will now to focus on meeting people's basic needs by developing the local collaborative economy and leveraging collaborations between the public, private, and commons sectors.

RESOURCES

- Regulation on Collaboration Between Citizens and the City for the Care and Regeneration of Urban Commons: comune.bologna.it/media/files/bolognaregulation.pdf

- LabGov's involvement in and perspective on the project: www.labgov. it/2014/12/18/bologna-regulation-on-public-collaboration-for-urban-commons

- CO-Bologna project online hub (Italian): www.co-bologna.it

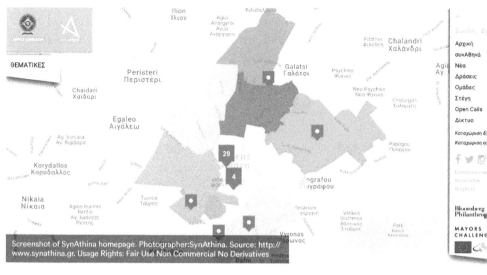

SynAthina:
Online Community Platform for Civic Projects

📍 Athens, Greece

—

By Ryan T. Conway

PROBLEM

Greece's ongoing financial instability has taken its toll on the country. A government debt crisis, exacerbated by Olympic-driven public-investments, created significant economic destabilization. Subsequent austerity policies, bailouts, debt restructuring, protests, riots, strikes, and leveled livelihoods have, together, reduced residents' faith in the national government. How can citizens organize themselves through alternative economies in order to meet their collective needs?

SOLUTION

In 2013, Amalia Zeppou, a documentarian and activist, approached the mayor of the city to promote self-organized solutions that had evolved to address the challenges facing Athens. Inspired by her vision, the mayor hired her as an adviser on civil society networking for the city, and she spearheaded the creation of a platform called SynAthina to connect all the local projects, to each other and to the city, as per a story in Citiscope. Soon after, Zeppou became Athens' Vice Mayor for Civil Society.

"We could have almost predicted the ideas that came in. What was more significant was that SynAthina broke the ice, and the tension among community groups in that area, helping them to collaborate. These groups saw that even though some of them didn't know each other – or if they did, they kind of didn't like each other – that their ideas for the neighborhood were actually quite similar."

Amalia Zeppou, Athens' vice mayor for Civil Society

Source: CityLab

SynAthina is an online community platform intended to engage civic projects across Athens. It allows citizens to map their activities, post events, and connect with volunteers and funders. Citizens or organizations can submit ideas for city improvements – from enhancing municipal services to changing city policies – and they can partner with the relevant civil servants, businesses, and nonprofits in order to implement innovations.

RESULTS

- In just the first phase of SynAthina, 120 grassroots groups listed over 500 projects and activities.

- In 2014, SynAthina was among the winners of the Bloomberg Philanthropies Mayors Challenge.

- By 2016, more than 1,000 projects were posted on SynAthina by over 200 of these self-organized civic groups. To share their innovations beyond Athens, SynAthina implements an evaluation mechanism, wherein the top 10 activities of each year are documented and translated into toolkits that any community can use.

RESOURCES

- SynAthina: www.synathina.gr

Block By Block:
Participatory Planning Using Virtual Worlds

◉ Nairobi, Kenya

By Ryan T. Conway

PROBLEM

Urban planning has historically relied on top-down processes in which technical experts create land-use designs that are then authorized by municipal officials. Even though international development agencies and many professional planners have endorsed the extensive research supporting participatory approaches, the wide variety of challenges that each urban planning project faces has made it difficult to establish transferable methods, even among wealthier cities in the world. How can organizations collaborate to create public spaces in impoverished areas such as the Kibera neighborhood in Nairobi?

SOLUTION

In 2011, Mojang – a video-game studio based in Stockholm, Sweden, founded by the creator of popular gaming platform Minecraft – partnered with the Swedish government to develop new tools for urban planning. Utilizing Minecraft, Mina Kvarter was introduced as a program to involve the tenants of nearly 1 million public-housing apartments in reconstructing and revitalizing their neighborhoods. The United Nations Human Settlements Programme or U.N. Habitat then partnered with Mojang to use similar methods

"It has proven to be a great way to visualize urban planning ideas without necessarily having architectural training. The ideas presented by the citizens lay as a ground for political decisions."

Carl Manneh, co-founder of Mojan

in the United Nations's Global Public Spaces Program that sought to upgrade 300 public spaces, starting in Nairobi.

The program, called "Block by Block," is primarily sponsored by Mojang. The company works with organizations like FyreUK, a Minecraft modelling group, to build the initial renderings. U.N. Habitat coordinates participatory design workshops for community groups, empowering them to alter the renderings in ways that reflect their real needs, and presents the results to city officials.

RESULTS

- In a study on the 15 projects – in 12 countries – completed through Block by Block, U.N. Habitat found that using the technology as a tool for participatory urban planning and design was "a powerful way to include nontraditional stakeholders in decisionmaking processes," and that "[v]isualization is crucial in how people perceive reality, and Minecraft is therefore useful for agreeing joint policy positions and solutions."

- Prototyped at the Undugu playground in Nairobi's Kibera neighborhood, the participatory method immediately proved useful, allowing residents and architects to collaboratively resolve design discrepancies and create a plan they could agree upon.

RESOURCES
- Block by Block: blockbyblock.org

Open Source App Loomio Used to Govern 200-person Artist Collective

◉ Hamburg, Germany

By Neal Gorenflo

Gängeviertel Collective emerged in 2009 following the occupation of 12 buildings in the center of Hamburg, Germany, next to the European headquarters of Google, Facebook, and Exxon-Mobile. The original motivation for the occupation was to create affordable space for local artists to live and work while saving the historic buildings from development. The collective is governed by a weekly general assembly which every member can attend, and where they can speak out, and vote. However, for more complex decisions requiring detailed preparation, the community uses Loomio, an open-source collective decision-making app created by the Loomio Cooperative. This online tool can quickly and easily take input from all community members and, after adequate feedback collection and deliberation on Loomio, bring the decision back to the main assembly for a final vote. The software was used for decisions about the potential ownership structure of the collective's housing and remodeling of the main gathering place.

RESOURCES

• Background on the collective: blog.loomio.org/2016/02/22/gaengeviertel

• Loomio app: www.loomio.org

Neighborhood Partnership Network:
Empowering Residents to Participate in City Planning

⌖ New Orleans, Louisiana, U.S.

By Ryan T. Conway

The aftermath of Hurricane Katrina revealed longstanding economic and racial inequalities in New Orleans, with low-income people of color having been left most vulnerable to the disaster. Even those who managed to escape the storm returned to find public services had become privatized, their housing demolished by developers, and their access to basic needs almost nonexistent. Amid the chaos, many people self-organized to support and provide mutual aid to each other. From this, the Neighborhood Partnership Network (NPN) emerged to empower residents to take part in city planning. Since 2006, the NPN has connected neighborhoods through regular meetings, a weekly newsletter, and a self-published journal. NPN has held a Capacity College that builds individual and organizational capacity through workshops and classes on topics ranging from stormwater management to filing public records requests. Furthermore, it was a pivotal advocate for pushing through changes to New Orleans' City Charter, which requires the city to implement "a system for organized and effective neighborhood participation in land-use decisions and other issues that affect quality of life."

RESOURCES

• Neighborhood Partnership Network: www.npnnola.com/about_npn

Club of Gdańsk:
Cross-Sector Collaboration for Urban Administration and Planning

♀ Gdańsk, Poland

⎯⎯

By Ryan T. Conway

While the port city of Gdańsk was ravaged by World War II, a majority of its population was either lost or displaced during its many years of heavy conflict. Today, however, the Polish city is a modern and vibrant urban center in eastern Europe. Having
only relatively recently caught up with other European cities in terms of economic
development, the city looked for ways to improve its quality of life. The city created
the Club of Gdańsk, an informal think tank for civil society groups and grassroots
organizers to collaborate with city leaders to design and develop the Gdańsk's long
term strategy. What began as an experiment in enabling bottom-up processes to
identify priority issues, eventually became a fixture of the city's administration. Core
to the Club's civil society and government members is their commitment to a set of
values, which includes transparency, self-determination, and "courage to act." Over
the years, the Club of Gdańsk has transformed the city and brought about a wave of
institutional reorganization supported by the city administration. It has successfully
involved tens of thousands of citizens and made them active co-creators of city policies.

RESOURCES
• Gdańsk case study: urbact.eu/sites/default/files/cs-03b_si-gdansk-f3.pdf

LiquidFeedback:
Free and Open-source Civic Engagement Software

◉ Wunstorf, Germany

—

By Ryan T. Conway

E-governance is the state's use of communication technology to provide information and services to the public. Many cities have successfully implemented such systems to give people access to ongoing policy discussions, provide input on local policies, or even make proposals for official consideration. Though these efforts can enhance civic engagement, the bulk of the digital consultation platforms are proprietary and, therefore, carry a hefty price tag that many cities cannot afford. LiquidFeedback is a collaborative decision making software that is both free and open-source. That means it is freely available for anyone to install, maintain, and modify – although they may need the help of a computer technologist to put it into place. The Public Software Group in Berlin had initially developed it for use within political parties and community organizations, but in 2015 they scaled it up to expand its application to e-governance. Since then, several cities in Germany and across Europe have incorporated LiquidFeedback into their digital consultation systems.

RESOURCES
• LiquidFeedback: liquidfeedback.org

Participatory Budgeting:
Collective City-making in Porto Alegre, Brazil

◉ Porto Alegre, Brazil

—

By Anna Bergren Miller with Marco Quaglia

Brazil's mid-20th century military dictatorship (1965-1985) concentrated political and economic power within the federal government, leaving municipal authorities with little authority over local housing and urban development. Meanwhile, a high degree of economic inequality combined with the absence of land-use regulations encouraged the proliferation of "favelas" and other informal settlements.

At the time of the democratic reforms of the late 1980s (including, crucially, the 1988 Federal Constitution), Porto Alegre, the capital of the Brazilian state of Rio Grande do Sul, boasted relatively high literacy and life-expectancy rates. According to the World Bank article, "Empowerment Case Studies: Participatory Budgeting in Brazil," one-third of its residents nonetheless lived in informal settlements, where they were cut off from access to city utilities and public health services.

To better the quality of life and health outcomes for city residents, and to accord with the new emphasis on democratization and decentralization, the incoming "Partido dos Trabalhadores" (Brazilian Workers' Party) municipal government introduced participatory budgeting to Porto Alegre, beginning in 1989.

The participatory budgeting process in Porto Alegre follows an annual cycle. In March or April, the city government presents a review of the previous year's investment plan. During April and May, citywide, regional, and neighborhood assemblies meet to establish priorities, elect councilors, and perform local-level budget reviews. In May and July, assemblies solidify priorities and elect delegates to participate in the funding request review process. New councilors begin work on a draft investment plan in July; the investment plan is made part of the city budget and presented at regional forums in late summer and early fall. During November and December, residents propose and consider revisions to the participatory budgeting statute itself. Approximately 50,000 residents decide (out of 1.5 million inhabitants) how approximately 650 million reals (nearly $200 million) is spent annually of the city's construction and services budget.

A 2008 World Bank study, "Brazil: Toward a More Inclusive and Effective Participatory Budget in Porto Alegre," concluded that participatory budgeting helped reduce poverty rates in Brazilian cities where it was instituted before 1996. The same study observed improved access to water and sanitation in all cities employing a participatory budgeting process.

A 2013 paper in "World Development" found that participatory budgeting did not increase the overall amount of capital spending by Brazilian municipalities, though it did change how those funds were allocated: cities using participatory budgeting tended to spend more on health and sanitation. Brazilian cities with a participatory budgeting process also saw a statistically significant decrease in infant mortality. The success of participatory budgeting in Porto Alegre has inspired 1,500 instances of participatory budgeting around the world. The Participatory Budgeting Project works to spread its use in the U.S. and Canada.

While effective, participatory budgeting faces some challenges. Per the World Bank case study mentioned above, the scope of participatory budgeting in Porto Alegre and other Brazilian cities is limited by the amount of funding dedicated to the process. Other challenges include uneven participation among different social groups, with those actors involved early on in the process (ex. low-income workers) overrepresented compared to newer demographics (ex. younger adults or the very poor).

VIEW THE FULL POLICY

- Here is the full text of and commentary on the City Statute of Brazil which puts participatory budgeting in the larger context of city administration in Brazil: www.ifrc.org/docs/idrl/945EN.pdf

RESOURCES

- Shareable's guide to starting participatory budgeting: www.shareable.net/blog/how-to-start-participatory-budgeting-in-your-city

- The Participatory Budgeting Project: www.participatorybudgeting.org

- Wikipedia page on participatory budgeting: www.internationalbudget. org/wp-content/uploads/Goncalves-Effects_of_Participatory_Budgeting-Brazil-2.pdf

Polycentric Planning for Climate Change:
Acting Locally, Aggregating Globally

📍 Dortmund, Germany

By Adrien Labaeye

Many believe that the only way to tackle climate change is through a global approach, but compliance to global emissions treaties is uneven and the system can be gamed. However, a 2009 World Bank working paper by Nobel Laureate Elinor Ostrom suggests that taking a "polycentric" approach might be more effective because it could reach more stakeholders, increase cooperation, and accelerate a response to climate change. Roughly speaking, a polycentric approach to climate change means a bottom-up, distributed effort lead by local, participatory multi-stakeholder groups that adds up to substantial change at a global level.

Such an approach is epitomized by Dortmund, Germany's Climate Protection and Energy Efficiency Consultancy ("Konsultationskreis Energieeffizienz und Klimaschutz") or "kek fora." According to the European Cultural Foundation's Build the City report, kek is designed to ensure broadly inclusive and participatory processes, involving city departments, utilities, business groups, nonprofits, and local citizens, all led by the city's mayor. ICLEI's case study #171, about Dortmund's energy transition work featuring kek, lists over 50 measures organized into six categories of action: energy efficiency, renewables and supply, efficiency retrofitting, community building and urban development, mobility, and cross-structural cooperation. The representative and coordinating functions of kek are essential. In only its first three years, kek completed 18 unique measures, initiated 34 new measures, and designed an energy transition master plan that seeks a 40 percent reduction in CO2 emissions by 2020.

RESOURCES

- World Bank working paper on a polycentric approach to climate change: https://openknowledge.worldbank.org/handle/10986/4287?show=full

- ICLEI's case study #171: www.iclei.org/fileadmin/PUBLICATIONS/Case_Studies/ICLEI_cs_171-Dortmund_2014_high-res.pdf

- Dortmund's energy transition master plan (German): www.dortmund.de/media/p/masterplan_energiewende_1/pdf_energiewende/Bericht_Masterplan_Energiewende.pdf

Shared Property Tax System Reduces Disparities in Public Services

♀ Seoul, South Korea

By Ryan T. Conway

A city's property tax system can worsen the gap between the rich and poor. Rich districts generate more funds for city services in their areas. Poor districts often get less services. Residents then sort themselves according to what areas they can afford, increasing disparities and thus tensions between groups. Can this vicious cycle of rich-getting-richer and poor-getting-poorer be broken so that all citizens can share equitably in the wealth and services of their city?

In 2008, Seoul implemented the Shared Property Tax System to address fiscal disparities between the city's 25 districts. As described in the research paper, "The Impact of the Shared Property Tax System on the Localities' Fiscal Capacity," all 25 of the city's districts contribute 50 percent of property tax revenues to a single pool, which is then redistributed in equal shares to the district governments. The paper suggests that the equal redistribution policy significantly reduced fiscal disparities among localities within the first four years. Another prominent example of property tax sharing is the Twin Cities of Minnesota, which implemented their scheme in 1971.

VIEW THE FULL POLICY

• legal.seoul.go.kr/legal/english/front/page/law.html?pAct=lawView&pPromNo=1321

RESOURCES

• Study on the impact Seoul's Shared Property Tax System: martin.uky.edu/sites/martin.uky.edu/files/Capstone_Projects/Capstones_2012/Kwon.pdf

• Article analysing fiscal disparities in cities: www.brookings.edu/blogs/the-avenue/posts/2015/04/02-ferguson-fragmentation-fiscal-disparities-katz-kneebone

• Book chapter analyzing taxes in cities: real.wharton.upenn.edu/~duranton/Duranton_Papers/Handbook/Taxes_in_cities.pdf

Ghent's Policy Participation Unit:
An Evolution of Public Engagement

♀ Ghent, Belgium

By Ryan T. Conway

The city of Ghent has a fairly long and developed tradition of citizen engagement. Advisory councils and public hearings, which were first introduced in the 1970s, evolved into more comprehensive approaches to community-based planning and led to the creation of a new city department, according to the city of Ghent. By 2003, that department began an "Area-Operation" that proactively interacts with neighborhoods in the 25 districts of the city.

This increased focus also produced a new name, the Policy Participation Unit, and includes 20 "neighborhood managers" who engage one or two of the districts and act as brokers between the city and residents to ensure consistent interaction, according to a report titled "Good Practices" published by the European Cultural Foundation in 2016.

The Policy Participation Unit also facilitates a Resident's Academy, grants for temporary-use projects in underutilized public spaces, neighborhood "Debatcafés" and focus groups, as well as a Neighborhood of the Month program that brings the mayor to each neighborhood for an entire month of interactive discussions.

VIEW THE FULL POLICY
- (Dutch) stad.gent/over-gent-en-het-stadsbestuur/stadsbestuur/ organisatiestructuur/bedrijfsvoering/dienst-beleidsparticipatie

RESOURCES
- European Cultural Foundation's publication on commons and culture: www.culturalfoundation.eu/library/build-the-city-book

Neighborhood Council Coalition:
Empowering Neighborhood Engagement

◊ Los Angeles, California, U.S.

—

By Ryan T. Conway

In the mid-1990s, Los Angeles faced some serious challenges: residents of the San Fernando Valley, the Harbor, and Hollywood had organized movements threatening to secede from the city. As reported by The Economist, The New York Times, The Atlantic and the The City Journal, organizers believed both that they received disproportionately fewer and lower-quality services from the city, and that the L.A. city administration paid too little attention to their needs.

The city sought to address these grievances by developing a system of greater representation that could also encourage greater civic participation. The 1999 City Charter amendment introduced a legally established Neighborhood Council System and a Department of Neighborhood Empowerment to support it (Article IX, Sec.900). Secession failed at the ballot and, by 2004, the details and legal ordinances of a Neighborhood Council System were developed and implemented.

Recent evaluations, such as the Yale Law & Policy Review or the University of Southern California Urban Policy Brief have revealed the need for improvement, but have also reported some success along with recommendations that the model be replicated in other cities. In fact, as described by Participedia, this has already begun to happen in cities like Nagoya, Japan and Memphis, Tennessee.

VIEW THE FULL POLICY

- Article IX: Department of Neighborhood Empowerment:
  http://www.coj.net/city-council/docs/consolidation-task-force/la-citycharter-neighborhooddept.aspx

RESOURCES

- Neighborhood Empowerment existing policies:
  empowerla.org/existing-policies

- Los Angeles Neighborhood Council Coalition: www.lancc.org

Participatory Urban Planning

♀ Auckland, New Zealand

By Marco Quaglia

Auckland's population is expected to grow by more than 50 percent in the next 30 years. To meet the social and infrastructural challenges associated with accelerated growth, in 2011 the city launched a comprehensive public consultation. The process included an open summit, public workshops, and multiple opportunities for the community to have a voice in the final outcome of their urban development plan. Eight thousand pieces of public feedback were submitted on the initial draft and were received through a variety of mediums and platforms such as the project's website, the postal service, email, and social media. The Office of Ethnic Affairs worked to solicit comments from ethnic minorities in order to make the final product as representative of the local community as possible.

The Auckland Plan is an example of a participative and inclusive co-design project that balanced market, state, and commons interests with the goal of becoming "the world's most livable city." Unique action plans have been developed for 13 key focus areas: People, Māori, Arts and Culture, Historic Heritage, Recreation and Sport, Economy, Environment, Response to Climate Change, Rural, Urban, Housing, Physical and Social Infrastructure, and Transport.

The Plan was finalized after a year of work, in which thousands of Aucklanders had the opportunity to give feedback, make proposals and draft their own submissions. Thanks to a transparent and honest system of communication between the city and civil society, the plan demonstrated a path of collaborative and co-managed design that is an example to be replicated in many cities around the world.

RESOURCES
• The Auckland Plan: theplan.theaucklandplan.govt.nz/

"

THE BEST WAY TO PREDICT THE FUTURE IS TO INVENT IT.

– ALAN KAY

ADVANCE PRAISE FOR SHARING CITIES

"Cities are the largest, most effective, and truly natural amalgamation of humans. Unlike nation states, cities are organic commons, which have evolved to circulate value and resources to its many members. Once again, Shareable shows how we can retrieve the very best features of urban life — consciously, constructively, and creatively."

— Douglas Rushkoff, author of "Throwing Rocks at the Google Bus: How Growth Became the Enemy of Prosperity" and host of the Team Human podcast

"If you're like me, you're frequently asked to back up your ideas with real-world examples. Here's a fantastic resource to do just that. Created by many of the world's leading sharing researchers and practitioners, it's a highly accessible collection of the most exciting and innovative cases of sharing and commoning now underway around the world. With excellent framing essays, "Sharing Cities" is indispensable for anyone interested in sharing, new economics, and system change. Make a space for it on your bookshelf."

— Juliet Schor, professor of Sociology at Boston College and author of "Plenitude: The New Economics of True Wealth"

"Seoul Metropolitan Government (SMG) has promoted Sharing City policies and projects since its declaration in 2012 as a Sharing City. However, learning from other cities has not been easy. This book, containing over 130 case studies and model policies from around the world, will help us and other officials, enterprises, and citizens striving to create Sharing Cities. The SMG hopes this book will spread around the world and help the Sharing Cities movement thrive."

— Mayor Park Won-soon, Seoul, South Korea

"In "Sharing Cities: Activating the Urban Commons," Shareable has crowdsourced a groundbreaking international compendium of sharing policies and practices that both inspire us with their vision and creativity, and call upon us to share much more, more widely, and more often. The diversity of sharing is impressive: from food to finance, from work to waste, each case is a tried and tested community-based solution. This is the essential roadmap to what is possible."

— Julian Agyeman, professor of Urban and Environmental Policy and Planning at Tufts University and co-author of "Sharing Cities: A Case for Truly Smart and Sustainable Cities"

"This is the book that urban commoners have been waiting for. The commons is not an utopia, but a concrete series of solutions to the challenges of the day, especially in the context of state and market failure. With the market state in deep crisis, cities offer a way forward, they can share successful commons-based solutions for housing, transportation, food, jobs, and help these practical solutions replicate across the globe. This is an inspiring snapshot of what we can already do, right now."

— Michel Bauwens, founder of the Foundation for Peer-to-Peer Alternatives

""Sharing Cities: Activating the Urban Commons" is a practical reference guide for community-driven solutions to key urban challenges such as affordable housing, sustainable mobility, and more. It showcases a real sharing economy that is spreading globally around the world in a pattern of people-powered "rhizomatic growth." Rhizomes are plants that are connected at the roots like bamboo. While you don't see the connectivity on the surface, it enables plants to share resources and keep every plant healthy. This is a metaphor for why Sharing Cities are the future and why nonprofits need to participate."

— Beth Kanter, trainer, speaker, and co-author of "The Happy, Healthy Nonprofit"

"There's a lot of facile talk lately about the sharing economy, but this book is about the real deal. It's not about multibillion dollar companies optimizing capital utilization, but about people-to-people approaches to actually sharing, forging community, and building commonwealth. More than 100 case studies and model policies provide an exciting glimpse and practical roadmap into the possibilities of cities as platforms — for growing the common wealth."

— Gil Philip Friend, chief sustainability officer at the City of Palo Alto, California, and inaugural member of the Sustainability Hall of Fame

"Optimistic, collaboratively created, with anticipation of ongoing evolution, this book provides examples of concrete forays into the new sustainable, equitable, and just economy we must and are building in cities."

— Robin Chase, co-founder and former CEO of Zipcar, author of "Peers, Inc."

"In this impressive collection of case studies from around the world, "Sharing Cities" showcases the enormous potential of urban commons to make cities more liveable, affordable, and convivial. A more hopeful future is already arriving! Now let's expand the infrastructures, policies, and projects to catalyze an even bigger surge of creative, bottom-up energies."

— David Bollier, director of the Reinventing the Commons Program at the Schumacher Center for a New Economics

"What if we shape a new urban lifestyle based on sharing? What cities are using sharing in urban development? "Sharing Cities" answers these questions with over 130 case studies from around the world that show a more rewarding and sustainable lifestyle is possible through sharing. The sharing solutions in this guidebook address common urban issues and offers a compelling vision of a true sharing economy."

— *Yuji Ueda and Daisuke Shigematsu, co-founders of the Sharing Economy Association, Japan*

"Cities are where we see signals of the future first, and what cities do today is likely to shape regions, nations, and the globe for the decades to come. "Sharing Cities'" collection of commons-based solutions from around the world provides a compelling vision of a more resilient, equitable, and convivial future city that's well within reach. It's essential reading for urban change agents and policymakers everywhere."

— *Marina Gorbis, executive director of the Institute of the Future, author of "The Nature of the Future"*

""Sharing Cities" is an awesome and inspiring collection that only a collaborative effort can bring about! It inspires us to heal the planet and ourselves through more sharing and commoning. It shows that there is no one blueprint, no one model, no one perfect enabling policy, but a diverse collection of well-designed policies and projects can help the urban common thrive."

— *Silke Helfrich, commons activists, co-editor of "The Wealth of the Commons"*

"With today's triple crises of sustainability, democracy, and equity, it's easy to feel overwhelmed and just sit on the couch waiting for some magic leader or invention for the answer. No need to wait any longer! "Sharing Cities" shows that the answer is us. It lays out a vision, with concrete examples, of how we can ease pressure on the planet, increase access to the things people need, and strengthen our democracy through sharing. Sharing may sound simple, but it's truly revolutionary in its potential to build a more healthy and just future for all. Read this book and let's get started building a better world."

— *Annie Leonard, executive director, Greenpeace USA and author of "The Story of Stuff"*

"By far the best single guide to the exploding commons revolution: Practical and revolutionary; immediate and far-seeing; a truly indispensable and fast-moving handbook on the change that is building community from the ground-up worldwide."

— *Gar Alperovitz, co-founder of The Democracy Collaborative and author of "What Then Must We Do? Straight Talk About the Next American Revolution"*

"Shareable's new book starts with a pivotal question, "How can we turn cities from impersonal engines of destruction into intimate communities of transformation?" Not only will you get answers, but you'll also get a better understanding of the systemic change required to transform our cities. It features the most creative commons-based solutions from around the world and shows that people-driven innovation is not a fad. Reading the cases gave me hope, and it will likely do the same for city innovators everywhere. Now let's make sure that all city officials and policymakers around the world get a copy of this book!"

— *Antonin Léonard, co-founder of OuiShare*

"There's long been a common dream of sustainable, equitable, convivial communities where people's strong connections with one another translate into great places for everyone to live. But now — in bits and pieces around the planet — it's becoming a reality. "Sharing Cities" is your handy guidebook to the exciting possibilities now surfacing. From an urban orchard in Boston to enabling legislation for sharing in Seoul to a bazaar governed by the principles of the commons in Hyderabad, India — this book will fortify your optimism with practical evidence."

— *Jay Walljasper, author of "All That We Share: A Field Guide to the Commons"*

""Sharing Cities" is a practical guide for those seeking to transform cities for the common good. This is not a book about big corporations in the so-called "sharing economy" — it's a book about the explosion of bottom-up, creative, collective action to change society by reviving the urban commons. The book's case studies and model policies show an inspiring yet pragmatic way forward that people everywhere need to know about."

— *Gabriel Metcalf, co-founder of City CarShare, author of "Democratic by Design"*

"Hundreds of cases, hundreds of stories of unique human beings whose strength is changing many people's lives in many cities around the world. One simple belief threads them together — that the urban commons will be a game changer in the 21st century."

— *Christian Iaione, Professor of Urban Law and Policy, Co-Director of LabGov*

ADDITIONAL PUBLICATIONS FROM SHAREABLE

How To: Share, Save Money & Have Fun (2016)

A collection of insightful guides on sharing housing, transportation, food, education, music and more. This book shows you how to lead a more enjoyable life, with your family and in your community, while saving money.

www.shareable.net/blog/how-to-share-save-money-have-fun

Policies for Shareable Cities (2013)

The guide curates scores of innovative, high-impact policies that US city governments have put in place to help citizens share resources, co-produce, and create their own jobs. It focuses on sharing policy innovations in food, housing, transportation, and jobs – key pocket-book issues of citizens and priorities of urban leaders everywhere. The guide is meant to help cities develop more resilient, innovative, and democratic economies.

www.shareable.net/blog/new-report-policies-for-shareable-cities

Share or Die (2012)

A series of forays into uncharted territory, this graphically rich collection of essays, narratives, and how-tos is an intimate guide to the new economic order and a must-read for anyone attempting to understand what it means to live within the challenges of our time.

www.shareable.net/share-or-die

Crowdfunding Nation (2011)

A collection of articles on crowdfunding's history, future, and its usefulness for social movements, how-to guides exploring the best practices for launching a campaign, the legal considerations of crowdfunding – and case studies of innovative and inspiring projects – and an interview with Kickstarter's Daniella Jaeger.

www.shareable.net/blog/crowdfunding-nation-ebook-now-available-in-epub-and-kindle-formats

Shareable Futures (2010)

In this collection of short stories and speculative essays, literary futurists imagine a world to come where technology has changed the rules of ownership and access, and people are able to share transportation, living spaces, lives, dreams, everything and anything. These are futures in which we are surviving and even thriving, largely by learning to share our stuff.

www.shareable.net/blog/shareable-futures

ABOUT SHAREABLE

Shareable is a nonprofit media outlet and action network that empowers people to share for a more resilient, equitable, and joyful world. We inspire social change by publishing stories, analysis, and tools in collaboration with our global partners.

Our work is based on the conviction that programs and policies that foster sharing, cooperation, and collaboration play a vital role in creating a sustainable and prosperous world for all.

You can connect with Shareable by subscribing to our weekly newsletter here shareable.net/newsletter, following us on Facebook.com/Shareable and Twitter.com/Shareable, and e-mailing us: info@shareable.net.

SERVICES:

Shareable provides a range of services to nonprofits, businesses, and governments worldwide including keynote speeches, workshops, consulting, site sponsorship, and editorial projects. To learn more about our services, please drop us a line: info@shareable.net.

CPSIA information can be obtained
at www.ICGtesting.com
Printed in the USA
LVHW010305091019
633524LV00021B/2181/P